Hannah's Forehead & Other Horror Stories

420 of 726

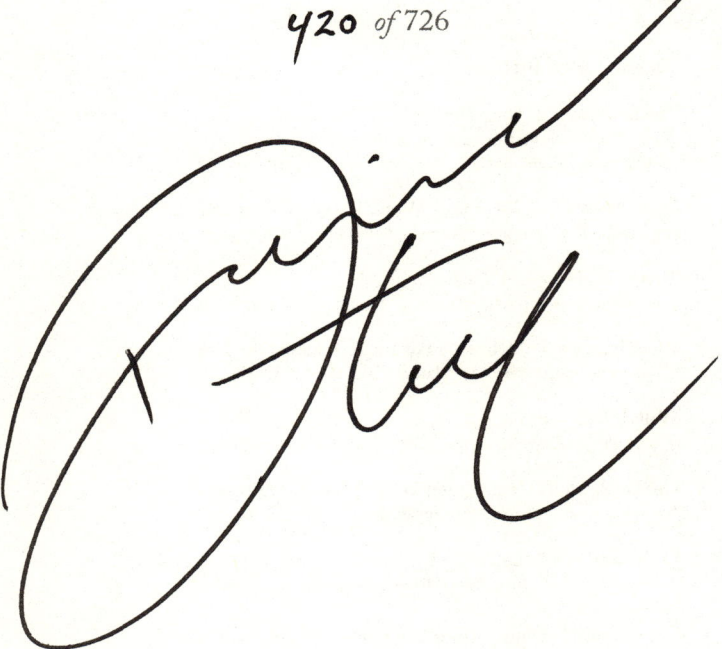

Copyright © David Thorne 2025 All rights reserved.

ISBN 979-8-9998913-0-3
HANNAH'S FOREHEAD & OTHER HORROR STORIES
LIMITED EDITION

DWFC: AUG18/260

www.27bslash6.com

This book is sold subject to the condition that it shall not, by way of trade or otherwise, be lent, re-sold, hired out, re-produced on the Internet or otherwise circulated without the author's prior consent in any form of binding or cover other than that in which it is published. This book may contain photos of bees. Colours may, in time, fade. Refrigerate after opening.

By the same author:

The Internet is a Playground
A *New York Times* bestselling book about overdue accounts, missing cats, and pie charts.

Look Evelyn, Duck Dynasty Wiper Blades, We Should Get Them
A book about design agencies, above ground pools, and magic tea.

That's Not How You Wash a Squirrel
A book about toasted sandwiches, sociopathy, and secret underground tunnels.

Wrap It In a Bit of Cheese Like You're Tricking the Dog
A book about suggestion boxes, buttons, and third-degree burns.

Walk It Off, Princess
A book about cantilevers, secret spots, and Antarctic expeditions.

Deadlines Don't Care if Janet Doesn't Like Her Photo
A book about fish people, office romance, and big red rocks.

Let's Eat Grandma's Pills
A travel book about frogs, buckets, and transparent bubble pods.

Just Because It Happened to You Doesn't Make It Interesting
A book about sleeping, static electricity, and blind fish that live in caves.

For Hannah

Thank you for everything you do. No, don't get up, I've got it.

Alternative Titles For This Book

A Mary Poppins Carpetbag of Surprises

Hit the Ground Complaining

Paragraphs From the Stupid Stuff Folder Without Context

The Joy Vacuum 5000

I'll Have Four Lobsters and a Gallon of Dom Perignon

Terms and Conditions

Got myself a Coke & I'll Be Rich Soon

Will You Need a Booster Seat For that?

Mild Umbrage Isn't An Energy

What's With the Font On the Cover?

Pointy Sticks and Where to Use Them

Oh, I Think He's Tired

Seeeeeeeeeeeb!

There's Plenty of Room On the Couch

Just Keep Chipping Away

Bang, Bang, Thud, Bang, Suki!

Contents

Introduction i
Hannah's Forehead 1
Benadryl / Docks 2
Skid Kids / Fitted Sheets 3
Water Parks 4
A Lot In Common / Neighbours 5
Hypocrisy / Florida 6
Empathetic 7
Spin Master / Subtitles 8
Conversation Tip #32 / Drop Bears 9
Bob-a-Job / Kneecapped 10
Neck Shoelace / Jesus 11
Backup Caps / Gender 12
Cape People / Junior Tennis 13
Gifts 14
Fame / Bag Cheese 15
Skin Care 16
Face Cancer / Lies 17
Monkey Being Dangerous 18
Captive Audience / Pepper Spray 19
Kimberly Drummond 20
Socks / Chores 21
Discipline / Mom & Pop Stores 22

The Eighties / Drugs	23
Pickle Juice / Babies	24
Hair Gel / Commemorative Coins	25
Bum Cancer	26
Vests / Bubble	27
Montana	28
Dinner Parties / Source	29
Landmark / Caterpillars	30
I (Almost) Got Away With It / Jello Shots	31
Triangles	32
The Main Bit / Hot Cheese	33
Arithmophobia	34
Fish / Spandexy	35
Short Men	36
Walkers / Honey	37
A Bit of a Show	38
Office Smokers / Jodhpurs	39
Wiener Dogs / E.Coli	40
Gary's Bottom	41
Show & Tell	42
Copper Wire / Tongue Drum	43
Deck Pics / Albanians	44
J.C. Penney / North Star	45
Small Talk / Language	46
Pretty Big Puddles / Dwarves	47
Pocket Knife People	48
Cruise Ships / 热狗	49

Memories / Be Best	50
Arizona / Smart Things	51
Ashley Furniture	52
Applebee's / Last Words	53
Reflective Glass / Moving	54
Sponge Rules / Instant Death	55
Chevrolet / Bats	56
Quick Trips / Playdate	57
Gravel	58
Lung Cancer / Ordinances	59
Trailers	60
Emma / Last Trip	61
Dr Phil / Rope	62
Dead Coworkers / Away Suitcases	63
Animals	64
Design Rule #72 / Sleep	65
Vape Oils / Seattle Real Estate	66
Bluetooth / Gazebo	67
Selling Brooms	68
Gary's Pants / Clippers	69
Blobby Wet Cheese / Gluten	70
Fireworks / Showers	71
Subaru Crosstrek	72
Hair In a Can / Diversity	73
Hobby Lobby / Karaoke	74
Creative Directors / Disability	75
Whistle / Letter to Graham's Mum Circa 1982	76

Magic / Goths	77
Philosophy	78
Peloton / Landscaping	79
Magnetism	80
Heather Locklear Ballerina Disney / Acid-Wash	81
Muscle Twinge	82
Splash / Parenting	83
Hacky Sacks / Thyroid	84
Mange / Gardens	85
Dave Matthews / Parent-Teacher Nights	86
Fire Pits / Pizza	87
Movies About Feet	88
Hit Men / Marketing	89
Factions	90
Agitation / Kayak	91
Christmas Rug	92
Dustpan Dustpan / Thoughts & Prayers	93
Girls Named Louise / Impressions	94
Breakups / New Orleans	95
Balloon Animals	96
Dollar General / Crimper	97
Robots	98
Exercise / Anne Frank	99
Gravy / Snake Bite	100
Magic Trick / Bumps	101
Television / Hentai	102
Amazon Reviews / Magnets	103

Physical / Omega 3	104
Piercings / Grapes	105
Dry Balls	106
Dumpster / Trophies	107
Trust British Paints?	108
Excel / Self Checkout	109
Adult Diapers	110
Maps / Shark Tank	111
Costumes	112
Moonraker / Couple's Costumes	113
Springs	114
Crabs / Lottery Winners	115
Gentle Ben	116
That's How You Get Nits / Bunkers	117
Teenage Pregnancy / Pictionary	118
One Upping / Adele	119
Shoplifting / Gums	120
Office Procedures / Bit Rude	121
Golf Balls / Coins	122
Bag Beans / Travel Cupboard	123
Paddleboards	124
M.A.S.H. / Body Language	125
Fence	126
Runaway / Swiffers	127
Ruse	128
School Notes / Cement	129
Immigration	130

Philadelphia / Interracial Couples 131
Lag 132
Coma / Spiral Binder 133
Yellow / Bezels 134
Air Freshener / Dancing 135
Again? 136
Pride Month / The Ashes 137
Bongo Song 138
Plank Partner / March 139
Winfield Blue / Cats 140
Autism 141
Covered Trailers 142
Banter / Guest Bags 143
Helmets / Ducks? 144
Checkouts / Therapy 145
Wranglers / England 146
Oil Changes 147
Man Cave 148
Some Kind of History / Adulting 149
Marooned 150
Secrets / Greenpeace 151
The Really Big Pumpkin 152
Farmers / Rumours 153
Elderly Clients 154
Germans Telling Jokes / Fondue Parties 155
Iwa-Bansu / Welding 156
Texting 157

Big Mug	158
Cloning / Home Projects	159
Pan Clangers	160
Leather Pants / Mr Steve	161
Chairs	162
Salt-Water Crocodiles / Time Travel	163
Tom's Rusty Hinge Story	164
Pottery Barn / How Was Your Day?	165
Children	166
Choices / Tripadvisor	167
Chevrons	168
Tall Grass / Itinerary	169
Hike / Dentist	170
Salty / Cargo Shorts	171
Math / Poutine	172
Wills / Hall & Oats	173
Wigs / Crows	174
Sinkhole / PTSD	175
Pharmaceuticals	176
Adhesive Nipples / Plumbing	177
ISIS	178
Dining Tables / Hulu	179
Aquaman's Mom	180
Facebook / Excuses	181
Log Cabins	182
Signs / The Classics	183
Magic Mushrooms	184

How Is That a Tango? / Spare Room 185
Wrong Number / Love Gun 186
The CEO of Levers 187
Old Blossom 188
Walter's Bike / Pointy Sticks 189
Night Wasps 190
Professor Television / Tin Tin 191
County Fairs / Magnification 192
Immortality / Golf 193
Product Research 194
Butter / Mr Mercury 195
Patterns 196
Carl / Slazenger 197
Mini-Stroke 198
Emergency / 800% Pleased 199
Outback Steakhouse 200
Homeless People / Nuhughn 201
Patchouli 202
Singing Bowls / Pho 203
Country Music 204
Once a Designer / Venmo 205
Poland 206
Large Properties / Apple II 207
Money Sock 208
Parking Pass / RV Adventure 209
Ayers Rock 210
Verizon / Party Invites 211

The Phantom	212
Board Games / Sleep Number	213
Home Haircuts	214
Boyfriend / Patrick Rafter	215
Proposal	216
Bandana / Consensus Bias	217
Hobbies	218
Monetization / Kip	219
Gourds	220
Tractors / Knots	221
Montreal / Lightning	222
Club Membership / Muppet Thing	223
Vet Bills	224
Dressups / Down Syndrome	225
Judgmental	226
Leg Room / Apps	227
Caterpillar Scientists / Floatie	228
Onions / Mr Chapman	229
Chewy	230
Social Distancing / Petrol	231
Personal Gifts / Poetry	232
Cats On the Counter / Judi Dench	233

Introduction

My offspring Seb isn't speaking to me at the moment. It's a fairly common thing; last year he didn't speak to me for two weeks because I trimmed his beard while he was sleeping. I did a good job, it's not like I gave him a donut-shaped goatee. The time before was after I hid in his closet - I didn't expect him to be naked when he opened it and I didn't jump-scare him, I just said, "Hello." That was only a week of not speaking to me as he eventually needed a ride to Walmart to buy thermal paste.

This time, it's because I asked his girlfriend Hannah, AKA the Joy Vacuum 5000, "What do you actually bring to the table?" It was during a vacation at a rented beach house, and while I'm known for my saint-like patience, a week of Hannah was just too much for me. I'm not saying she ruined the vacation... actually, yes I am. A week in a damp hole would have been more fun. It's not just that Hannah is loud, lazy, and completely indifferent to anyone else's comfort or needs, she's also a pouter. Everyone's entitled to a pout now and then, but Hannah's pouting is unrelenting. It's not the adult version of pouting, the one where you make yourself a coffee without asking if anyone else wants one, it's the toddler version where you jut out your bottom lip and make a face like you're pushing out a difficult poo. Sometimes Hannah's lip-jut-poo-push face is the result of an understandable annoyance, such as having to ride an orca floatie when she wanted the duck, but I've also witnessed it while she was riding an ATV. Who sulks on an ATV? It's impossible not to have fun on an ATV, it's a scientific fact. It's also a fact that cute girls get a 'princess pass' - life is easier when you're attractive so even minor issues can be traumatizing - but Hannah isn't attractive so she doesn't get a pass for anything.

"What's the issue, Hannah?"
"Nothing."
"What's with the face then?"
"What face?"
"The lip-jut-poo-push face."
"What?"
"That's what I call it. It's dreadful. Please cover your head with a towel so I don't have to look at it."

I have no idea what Seb sees in her, on a scale of 1 to 10 she's probably a 2, and she only gets that because she's not in a wheelchair and has all her teeth. I've seen close-up photos of bugs with better looking heads. Okay, maybe that's a bit of an exaggeration, she does have a large forehead though. When Seb first showed me a photo of her, I thought it was a picture of a butternut squash with a face drawn on it.

Of course, the **adult thing** to do would be to apologise to Seb for being rude to his girlfriend, and to let him know that I understand any disapproval I show towards her is a reflection on him and his decision to be with her... OR, I could release a limited edition book and call it *Hannah's Forehead and Other Horror Stories* because I think it's funny.

Seb will also think it's funny but he'll pretend not to so Hannah doesn't pout. I'll probably get a text from him that says, "Wow" with an angry face emoji. It's kind of like when Will Smith had to slap Chris Rock for mentioning his wife's bald head. You could tell Will was having a bit of a chuckle until he glanced at his wife and she gave him the 'you're in big trouble for laughing' look. Instead of shouting, "Keep my wife's name out of your mouth," he should have said, "Lol, do one about her fucking Jaden's friend." Really, Seb should thank me for drawing Hannah's forehead smaller on the cover image than it actually is.

At this point you may be wondering what the *Other Horror Stories* are and hoping they're not just bits from my earlier books. No, it's much worse than that.

Each time I release a new book, I don't just sit in a room and write pages, I write short paragraphs throughout the year and save those paragraphs to a folder titled

Stupid Stuff. Then, when it comes time to write a book, I'll search through the *Stupid Stuff* folder for paragraphs that can either be expanded on, or included somewhere with context. This book contains paragraphs from the *Stupid Stuff* folder without context. Some have never made it out of the *Stupid Stuff* folder before, some have but in different form. I could have called this book *Paragraphs From the Stupid Stuff Folder Without Context*, but it's not overly catchy and it wouldn't have annoyed Hannah. Regardless, 726 copies of this book now exist and you're holding one of them. Little effort for little outcome, but you should be used to that by now. Just sell it on eBay when I'm dead.

Also, I should note that this book doesn't contain *all* the paragraphs from the *Stupid Stuff* folder, as a lot of them don't make sense. I don't even remember writing half of them. One just says, "Hide all the bananas before Seb sees them." and another is about a shirt my coworker Ben once wore to work. Apparently I had an issue with the collar. I also had an issue with a chubby guy named Barry in 2007 and wrote about him rolling through his village and becoming a singularity point. There's even a poem which goes:

The View From My Bed A Poem by Barry
I have two buckets, green and blue.
On Tuesdays a nurse comes and cleans my poo.

I'm not sure what Barry did to annoy me so much. If I knew his last name, I'd send him an email and ask him. Here's a picture of his face Photoshopped onto a fat kid riding a scooter. If you recognise Barry, let me know. I think he worked at a box factory.

Hannah's Forehead

My offspring Seb definitely has a type. His first girlfriend had an astonishingly large forehead. People would stop and stare, children would cry. It was the type of forehead a cartoon mastermind might have, but bigger and zittier. Seb's second girlfriend's forehead was even bigger. You could land a drone on it, the type that leaves packages. His current girlfriend, Hannah, has a final boss forehead - like if you were playing a video game where you had to defeat the forehead people, Hannah would be at the end. I realize you're probably thinking, 'Oh come on, it can't be *that* big,' but you're wrong, it accounts for half her height. Here's a drawing **to scale** and not exaggerated in any way.

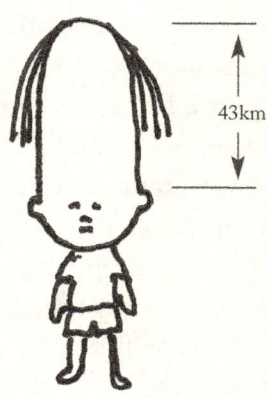

Benadryl

Holly's parents, Tom and Maria, take their cats on vacation with them. The cats sleep the entire trip as Maria gives them eight Benadryl tablets each. One of the cats died on their last trip, it's buried beneath on a grassy knoll behind a Burger King in Ohio. There's also one buried behind a Wendy's in Kentucky, a pumpkin farm in Tennessee, and a Rest-Inn motel in Florida. The one in Florida didn't die from an overdose, it chewed through a lamp cable and electrocuted itself while Tom and Maria were at an alligator feeding show.

Docks

2,830 people were electrocuted while swimming last year. That's a global number, so it's a lot less than were killed by falling off a ladder, but it's still pretty high. Apparently it's common around boat docks; one issue with the ground wire and anyone swimming is zapped. It's not a quick zap either, it's just keeps zapping and you drown while being zapped. It's like two horrific deaths in one. There's no way to really test for it either, apart from not being the first in or maybe throwing a bit of bread in and seeing if it sizzles. That might work.

Skid Kids

There were tennis courts at the end of the street I lived on as a kid. My friend Michael and I regularly rode our bikes there because the court surface was excellent for doing skids on. We called ourselves the Skid Kids - Michael was Skidmaster and I was Skidmarker. We were eventually banned from the courts, because of the marks, but we still rode there, we just made sure the gates at both ends were open in case we needed to make a quick getaway.

Fitted Sheets

Whenever my partner Holly changes our bedsheets, she asks me to help. How is changing sheets simplified by two people doing it? It isn't, it's more complicated as you have synchronise the fitted sheet tuck bit. It's a bit of together time though I suppose, plus the small things add up and you can trade them for big things.

"Let's go out."
"What?"
"We should have a date night."
"But I helped carry in the groceries yesterday."

Water Parks

I know a girl named Heather who started dating two weeks after her husband Ian drank a mango margarita too fast and had brain freeze so bad he died. Everyone's different, but don't post on Facebook that you've lost the love of your life and then post photos of you and some guy named Bob kayaking on a lake a week later. Apparently they met at a water park. Which just raises more questions.

"All I'm saying, Holly, is that if you died, I wouldn't immediately go to a water park."
"Maybe she needed cheering up."
"There's a grace period where you're not meant to be cheered up."
"And do what? Just sit in your house being sad?"
"Yes, staring out of a window or something."
"I wouldn't want to be alone, I'd want people around."
"Sure, people you know, not people in line with you to go down the Double Dipper Hydroslide. Would *you* go to a water park if I died?"
"No, I don't like water parks. I'd rather go zip-lining."

It's nice to know Holly won't be moping I suppose, bit hard to mope while you're zip-lining through a forest canopy with your new friend Kev.

A Lot In Common

My coworker Jodie is dating a woman twice her age with an Elvis haircut. I asked Jodie what she sees in her, apart from maybe a father figure, and she stated, "We have a lot in common; we both like music." No genre was specified, just music in general, which is like saying I have a lot in common with Jeff Bezos because we both wear pants.

"Everyone, I'd like you to meet my new girlfriend."
"That's a stick."
"And? We have a lot in common."
"Such as?"
"We spend a lot of time outdoors. We met in a park."

Neighbours

Don't wave at me when I'm taking out my trash, Ian. We're not friends. Your dog barks constantly and your backyard looks like the internment camp in *District 9*. Do a dump-run and buy a shock-collar. I don't care if it's cruel, after hearing your dog bark for eight hours straight, I'd happily zap it in the face with a cattle prod.

Hypocrisy

This morning, Kate, our HR manager, asked me, "Could you try to be more likable?" This implies that I'm unlikeable. I am, I accepted the fact long ago, but it was still a personal attack and there's no difference between her statement and my response of, "Could you try to be less wrinkly?" If I'm being written up, so should she, but apparently it's 'constructive criticism aimed at fostering a healthy environment' when HR makes personal comments, and a 'policy violation' when anyone else does. It would take a great deal of personal effort on my part to be likable, whereas all she has to do is stop raising her eyebrows so much. I refuse to be likable at all today. My coworker Gary just stated that his cat might need to be put down and I said, "Good", so we have Kate to thank for setting the mood.

Florida

Holly and I once had our vehicle broken into while we were staying at a hotel in Florida. They took our fold-up chairs and we had to sit on towels at the beach like unemployed people. I'm never going to Florida again; too many thieves and fat girls wearing Supreme® caps.

Empathetic

My coworker Gary just learned that he has the choice of putting down his cat or paying 4K for an operation to remove a tumor on its spine. As such, I thought it would be empathetic to send him the drawing below. According to Gary, it wasn't empathetic and he doesn't believe it was intended as such. Things were said which I expect an apology for. It's a perfect example of why it's pointless attempting to do anything nice for anyone around here.

Also, Walter, our junior designer, stated, "Please, you're not empathetic." When I countered that I was probably the most empathetic person in the office, he said, "Go on then, move something with your mind."

Spin Master

When I was eleven, I practiced breakdancing moves for two weeks and put on a show for my classmates during recess. I took a large piece of cardboard to school to spin on and asked everyone to call me Spin Master. The cardboard was from a washing machine box and Cathy Morris called me Spin Cycle.

Subtitles

My coworker Jason is a bit of a dickhead. He's the type that says *pfft* if you admit you don't buy organic free-range eggs from farmers who play the tongue drum to their chickens. He's also a fan of foreign films.

"Have you seen *Hgheú Oân Tchâio*? It's pretty much my favorite movie by acclaimed director Chói Hzgú. He films everything on a 1967 Honeywell Elmo Super Filmatic 104 camera upside-down through cheesecloth. His first film, *Ngângut*, is forty-six hours long.
"No, I like movies with spaceships in them."
"Of course you do. Well, if you'll excuse me, I have a gluten protest to attend. We're going to dress up as loaves of bread and block traffic."

Conversation Tip #32

If you run out of things to talk about with someone, ask them what their favourite mushroom is. Everyone has a favourite mushroom, even if it's just the Portobello. My favourite mushroom is the Giant Puffball.

Drop Bears

Everything in Australia that's not a spider has a spider on it, in it, or under it. We have spiders the size of small children which chase you on hiking trails; they live in holes with a secret door and know to wait until you're several steps past and looking the other way before they run out and wrap themselves around your leg.

"American?"
"Yes, we're visiting for the week. Planning to take in a few hiking trails."
"Nice. Do you own kevlar pants?"
"No, will we need them?"
"You should be fine. Just walk back-to-back and carry a pointy stick. Also, keep an eye out for drop bears."
"Ha, there's no such thing, is there?"
"Technically no, we just call them bears because they're big and furry. They're actually spiders."

Bob-a-Job

My parents made me join the Boy Scouts when I was ten. I hated it so I convinced my friend Matthew to join. Misery loves company and I hadn't made friends with any of the kids in my troop - most were older and had lots of merit badges. I had one badge, for traffic awareness, which is one more than Matthew had. He eventually earned around three hundred badges and needed to wear a special sash, but I was out by then. I learned the Scouts have something called bob-a-job, where you have to weed old people's gardens, so I told my parents the scoutmaster kissed my neck.

Kneecapped

I'm not a fan of the aisle seat on planes. I have ostrich legs which don't fit behind the seat in front of me unless they're splayed, so sitting in the aisle seat means I risk being kneecapped by the refreshments trolley. It's only happened once, but it was a solid hit, right in that little dip in the knee between bones that sends an electrical jolt up your spine and into your head. I was nodding off when it happened and screamed. I thought we were crashing.

Neck Shoelace

My friend JM doesn't own a tie. For formal events, he wears something called a Bolo tie, even though he's not a landowner in a Western film. It's basically a neck shoelace and I have no idea if it's just for decoration or functional in some way.

"Is that a shoelace around your neck?"
"Yes, it's a convenient way to carry a spare."
"But you're wearing boots."
'It's handy for other things. Like rappelling down very small cliffs or hog-tying a child."
"And why do you have a sock taped to your forehead?"
"Where do you keep your spare sock?"
"I don't carry a spare sock."
"Wow. Okay."

Jesus

"And then Jesus flew to the moon and collected rocks and flew back to Earth and built a pizza oven out of them."
"Gosh, Jesus is so awesome. He invented pizza?"
"Yes, and laminate flooring."

Backup Caps

I'm not a cap person. Some people can put on and take off caps all day because they have the right hair. For me, putting on a cap is a commitment. Once it's on, it's staying on. I don't have the kind of hair you can ruffle after taking off a cap; it goes flat and I look like one of those mental patients who wear their pants really high and masturbate constantly. On the odd occasion when I do wear a cap, perhaps camping or on a boat, I make sure I have two additional caps in case I lose the first cap. The third cap is the second cap's backup, but if I lose the second cap, it's time to go home. I should probably have three spare caps, but that's a lot of caps to be carrying about.

Gender

I thought I knew a transgender woman named Brooke once. Turned out she wasn't transgender and had no idea what I was talking about when I casually brought up gender reassignment surgery one day. I'd been open-minded and accepting for three years, so I was a bit annoyed that it was a complete waste of effort.

Cape People

I can generally put up with other people for about two hours. The time varies and is dependent on factors that may seem random and are. Having to justify my actions is one. I once left a party because a guy was wearing a cape. I'm not talking about a superhero cape, that would have been acceptable, I'm talking about the velvet-lined type people wore in England before everyone decided it looked stupid and stopped. I have no idea why he was wearing a cape and I don't care; I'm not hanging around cape people. They're the same type of people who blend their own vape-oils and can name all the Hobbits.

"Interesting point, but don't forget Bibbitypop poured drinks from a large wooden ladle."
"I do believe you're correct. But that would mean…"
"Exactly. There must have been *two* large wooden ladles at the Feast of Merriment in Stickshire."
"So many levels."

Junior Tennis

A boy on my under-twelves tennis team, named Steven, showed me how to perform cunnilingus by sticking his tongue in a condom he found at a bus stop.

Gifts

For my birthday last year, Seb and Holly gave me a cap with a built-in flashlight and a pair of really thin socks; I think the socks were the free ones women use to try on shoes in department stores. The year before, Holly gave me a gift card. I can't even remember what store it was for. It might have been J.C. Penney. I think Seb got me fish food. It's as if they have an secret contest to see who can get me the lamest present. There's probably rules, like it can't just be a piece of paper with the letter H on it, but anything between that and a backscratcher shaped like a skeleton's hand goes.

"It's David's birthday next week."
"Game on."
"The socks are going to be hard to top."
"Yes, but I have a couple of ideas. Which is worse, a USB powered coffee mug or a book about owls?"
"They're both about equal."
"What are you getting him?"
"A packet of drinking straws."
"The bendy type?"
"Pfft. No."
"Nice."

Fame

My father was on the news once. A Channel 9 News crew was doing a story about petrol-pump prices spiking over the Easter weekend, and my father was filling up our station wagon at the time. He was asked if the price hikes affected him and he replied, "Yes, because I've got an 18-gallon tank." He rang my mother and told her to tape it, but she taped the Channel 7 News instead. They had a fight about it and he accused her of doing it on purpose because she was jealous.

Bag Cheese

I have no idea how to catch a bus. I think there's some kind of numbering system but I don't know what the numbers mean. And how do you pay? Does the bus driver take credit cards? Do you have to tip? The last time I rode on a bus, the driver picked everyone up from my friend JM's house. That was a pretty small bus though, more like a big van really. JM took a bag of cheese for the journey and offered me some, but I don't eat bag cheese.

Skin Care

I know a woman named Sarah who looks seventy but dresses like a sixteen-year-old. Apparently she's only thirty-nine, but she's been thirty-nine for seventeen years. She's well past the point where people state, "Wow, she looks rough for thirty nine," so eventually she's going to have to turn forty. I tell everyone I'm sixty because I'd much rather have people asking what my secret to younger looking skin is than have them think, "So that's what happens when you only drink coffee and no water for forty years."

"Damn, you don't look sixty, David. What's your secret to younger looking skin?"
"Dryer lint and mayonnaise."
"What?"
"A one-to-one ratio. I mix it together in a blender and wear it as a mask for ten minutes. The micropolyamides in the lint activate the crotinials in the mayonnaise, which super-hydrates the top six layers of derma."
"Really?"
"Yes, you should try it."
"I will."

Face Cancer

My family had a 21" Rank Arena television set when I was young. If you sat close, you could see the images were made of red, green, and blue blobs, but you weren't meant to sit close, because televisions gave you face cancer. I think everything gave you face cancer back then. That's the problem with kids nowadays; not enough face cancer. There's no reason for them not to spend hours staring at screens. I didn't have any screens of my own, I had to create my own entertainment. I made outfits for sticks and pretended they were the little humans from *Land of the Giants*.

Lies

I'm not overly adept at coming up with lies on the spot. I understand the key is to keep the lie simple, but for some reason I always panic and add extra details. I once told a client his deadline was missed because I was in a Bangladesh kite-fighting accident. I wore a bandage to our next meeting and told him my sister was married to a man from Bangladesh named Hububu who she'd met overseas while researching constitutional republics.

Monkey Being Dangerous

My friend Geoffrey took up painting recently and he's surprisingly bad at it. His latest effort is of a knight in armour standing on top of a mountain raising his sword to a stormy sky. Apparently it's a self portrait, but the face looks more like a monkey. He named it *Journey's End* but I renamed it *Monkey Being Dangerous*.

"The title doesn't make any sense. The monkey is going to have to eventually walk back down the mountain, so you should have called it *Journey's Half Way Point* or *That Was a Bit Pointless, Good Exercise Though*."
"It's not a monkey and the journey is over because it was one of discovery. The fact he has to go back down afterwards doesn't come into it. Also, he doesn't need to walk, he can ride his horse."
"Where's the horse?"
"It's behind that rock. You can see its head sticking out a little bit."
"Oh yeah. I can kind of see the horse's body as well. Is the rock semi-transparent?"
"No, I painted the horse first but it didn't look right so I painted the rock over it but the horse was black so it shows through a little bit. I should go over it again."
"Or you could just rename the painting *Journey to the Semi-Transparent Rock*."

Captive Audience

One of our older clients refuses to discuss changes via email. I have to drive to his office for even the smallest amendments. Yesterday, I sat in traffic for two hours because he wanted to change the word 'and' to 'and/or' on a brochure about aural hygiene. The meeting took an hour, it always does, as I suspect a captive audience is his only means of social interaction.

"I met my wife in 1976 at a farmer's market. She was selling peas."
"Okay, and how is that relevant to earwax buildup?"
"It isn't. I had a moustache back then, as was the fashion…"

Pepper Spray

I saw a video about soldiers being pepper sprayed recently. After being sprayed, they had to pick up a big tire and put it over a pole. There was probably a point to this, there had to be, but if I were in the army and someone said to me, "We're going to pepper spray you and then we want you to put a tire over a pole," I'd steal a Jeep and make a run for it.

Kimberly Drummond

When I was twelve, my best friend Dominic had a massive crush on Dana Plato - the girl who played Kimberly in the television show *Diff'rent Strokes*. He had a poster of her on his wall which was signed "To Dominic, I love you, Kimberly." I was with him when he bought the poster at Target, so I know she didn't sign it herself. Also, if she had actually signed it, when he met her on a bus as he claimed, she would have used her real name, not the name of her character in the show.

"Did you watch *Diff'rent Strokes* last night?"
"No."
"You missed a good episode. Kimberly got her first bra."
"Did she?"
"Yes. If I was Willis, I'd fuck Kimberley. She's not his real sister. Do you sometimes wish you could jump into a girl's body, like take over her mind, and then go to your house and knock on the door and when you answer say, 'It's me, I'm in this girl's body. Quick, lets have sex?'"
"Um... no."
"No, I don't either. I was just asking if you do."

Socks

Holly never packs enough socks when we go on vacation and has to wash worn pairs in the bathroom sink. What's the point of having a nice hotel room if there's socks hanging everywhere to dry? We ordered room service once and when the guy wheeled the tray in, he said, "I'll just leave it here, under the socks." so it isn't just me.

Chores

While carrying a garbage bag to the curb this morning, the bag ripped. There were maggots in it, and I don't do maggots, so I made my offspring clean it up.

"Why do I have to do it?"
"Because it's one of your chores."
"You can't just add chores as you feel like it. Yesterday you added cushion fluffing to the list."
"The cushion was very flat."
"No it wasn't."
"Yes it was. You should make sure the cushion is fluffed after you use it. For the next person."
"I've never seen you fluff a cushion after you've used it."
"No, because it's your chore."

Discipline

My parents weren't big on discipline. The only physical punishment I recall receiving was having my mouth washed out with soap after calling my father a cocksucker. The worst part of the punishment wasn't the taste, it was that the only soap available was a mushy blob stuck to the shower floor. I remember thinking, as I spat the soap and a toenail into the sink, 'Nobody in our family has short curly hair, whose hair is this? Is it eyebrows?'

Mom & Pop Stores

I'm a big fan of Starbucks. I understand the issue with corporations driving out 'mom & pop' stores, but if mom and pop don't have three stores within a five-mile radius of wherever I am at all times, maybe they need to rethink their business model.

"It's not looking good, Edith. We've only sold four coffees this month and are on the verge of bankruptcy. As such, I've decided to diversify our offerings by investing our remaining life-savings in fidget spinners."
"Fidget spinners?"
"Yes, they're very popular."

The Eighties

The eighties weren't as colourful and fun as people make them out to be; everything was brown and almost everything you did got you molested. Ride your bike to the park? Molested. Sleep at a friend's house? Molested. I was molested on a ferry once.

Drugs

I've never really been into drugs. The fear of making a spectacle of myself has always been stronger than the desire to be high. Perhaps I should just 'loosen up a bit' as has been suggested, and inject heroin into my eyeballs, but at this point in my life I'd rather spend the money on plants.

"Okay, well I'm off. Have a good weekend, David."
"You too. Anything exciting planned?"
"Yes, I'm attending a rave in a forest. Bassnectar is playing. I'm going to take a lot of drugs and have sex with girls wearing furry boots. What about you?"
"I'm going to plant a birch."
"Nice."
"Yes, I'm a big fan of the birch."

Pickle Juice

Holly's mother, Maria, has three hobbies; sitting, smoking, and mulling. She's happiest sitting in her garage smoking with the roller-door up, occasionally entering the house to admonish her husband Tom for something she imagined him doing forty years earlier.

"I know you tried to poison me with pickle juice, Tom."
"What?"
"Pickle juice has a very distinctive taste."
"I have no idea what you're talking about and pickle juice isn't poisonous."
"That's hardly the point. You handed me a glass of water and I remember taking a sip and thinking, 'Hmm, this water is a bit pickley.'"
"When?"
"1984. We were watching *Webster*. It was the episode where Webster had his tonsils taken out."

Babies

When I was five, I asked my cousin Darryl where babies come from, and he told me they were shot out of t-shirt guns at basketball games.

Hair Gel

My mother used to cut my hair when I was young. She used a mixing bowl and ruler and I looked like I was wearing a motorcycle helmet. I pleaded with my parents to buy me hair gel, but my father explained it was only for two types of people:

"Do you think about other boy's penises?"
"What? No."
"Are you a synthesizer player in a British pop band?"
"No."
"Well, there you go. You don't need hair gel; your hair looks fine. The edges are perfectly straight and it hides your forehead and ears."

Commemorative Coins

Who keeps buying commemorative coins? There has to be a market for them, otherwise there wouldn't be so many television commercials. I saw one recently commemorating seventy years of Nascar - it was 'guaranteed to become a priceless family heirloom'. Kind of a shitty heirloom. It's like leaving someone a Fossil watch in your will.

Bum Cancer

Holly's father Tom was diagnosed with bum cancer recently. He had surgery last week to remove a small section of colon, but complications during the operation meant they had to remove the whole thing. He's always been a belligerent old fuck, now he's a belligerent old fuck with a bag of poo strapped to his side. While a bit of outrage is to be expected after a surprise-colectomy, Tom has actually gone more for the 'obey my every command for I am sans-colon' approach. He texted Holly at 3am last night demanding she bring him three cheeseburgers and a phone stylus. He also asked why I haven't been to visit him in the hospital yet - which is a bit rude. Like I don't have better things to do than go see his poo bag?

"Summon everyone to my bedside immediately!"
"You're not dying, Tom."
"No, but it's poo bag changing time and everyone needs to see how it's done."
"Why? It's your poo bag."
"No, it's *our* poo bag. Also, tell David to bring me a roll of yellow electrical tape, a signed copy of *Tanks* by Richard Ogorkiewicz, four safety pins, and a photo of a bridge."

Vests

Apparently when women give birth, there's some kind of chemical released in the brain that blurs the whole event and makes them think pushing a human out of their body wasn't horrific. Camping must release the same chemical. Once you're home and in your comfy pants watching Netflix, the memory of all the lifting and carrying things fades away. Also, camping looks fun in L.L.Bean catalogues and you'll probably flip through a couple before your next camping trip and think, "I should buy a vest." I own five vests and have never worn any of them. If I'm looking for a jacket in my wardrobe and come across a vest, I think, "It's cold outside so something with sleeves would be better."

Bubble

My coworker Gary has old man head flakes. I assume it's just dandruff, but I've never seen dandruff the size of cornflakes before. I once witnessed a flake drift down, like a cartoon leaf, and land in his coffee. It floated for a bit and, when it finally sank, a bubble popped up. Where did the bubble come from?

Montana

If I ever decide to write a romance novel, the main character will be a girl named Cadence who is in a wheelchair due to a horse-riding accident. Her romantic interest will be a shy but handsome inventor named Jackson. In the end, he'll build Cadence a robot suit so she can ride again.

"Wouldn't she be too heavy to ride a horse if she's wearing a robot suit?"
"I haven't worked out all the details yet, just the premise and their names. I'll probably set it in Montana."
"She could probably ride a horse without a robot suit. The inventor could just add straps to a saddle. Is the girl a paraplegic or can she use her arms?"
"It doesn't matter now; you asked too many questions and I become disillusioned with the whole thing. I'll make it about a female concert pianist who loses a hand in an elevator accident instead."
"Is her love interest going to build her a robot hand so she can play again?"
"No, he also has a missing hand and he secretly learns to play the piano so they can play her favourite song together."
"Are they missing the same hand or opposite hands?"

Dinner Parties

I'm not a fan of eating at other people's houses. Firstly, you don't know what their 'cat on the kitchen counter' rule is. Secondly, everything else. Having to take a bottle of wine, standing in the kitchen, anecdotes about mattresses, staring at each other across the table after the meal is finished. I just want to pay a check and leave. There should be a dedicated section on Yelp where you can leave reviews for dinner parties.

★☆☆☆☆ **Meh**

I should have taken a cheaper bottle of wine. Cathy needs to add more salt to her cooking and her windows could do with a good wash. Also, Robert's anecdote about getting his car serviced went for too long and not everyone likes Pictionary.

Source

My coworker Gary filed a formal complaint against the guy who delivers our office cooler water bottles this morning. Gary asked him if the water was sourced from a spring or produced through reverse osmosis, and the guy replied, "How the fuck would I know?"

Landmark

There's a pub in Adelaide called The Grace Emily. It's sticky, and dirty, and so are the people who drink there. I once saw a woman wax her armpits at the bar. Someone stuck one of the hairy wax blobs on a window and it's been there so long, it's become a landmark.

"Where's Bob?"
"Left of the hairy wax blob."

Caterpillars

My coworker Gary filed a formal complaint against me this morning for saying his ears look like caterpillars. In my defense, Gary's ears are astonishingly hairy - and I didn't say his ears look like caterpillars, I said it looked like he was wearing caterpillar earrings. I also stated that his ear hair adds three feet to his width and if he ever gets bored working at the agency he could find alternative employment at a carwash as one of the brushes. I don't just go around critiquing ear hair for no reason though; we were in a meeting and Gary kept asking people to speak up. It's like wearing sunglasses inside and complaining about how dark it is.

I (Almost) Got Away With It

I watched a television show last night about a guy who got caught with drugs in his bum and spent ten years in a Turkish prison. He had to share a room and a poo bucket with thirty other guys. There's no way I could poo in a bucket with thirty guys watching. I'd just hold it in until I died.

Jello Shots

Melissa, our front desk human, lost her license recently. She still drives, but only when there are lots of other cars around her. For Melissa, it's not about legality, it's about risk vs. catching a bus. I get it, there's no way I'd catch a bus to work, but maybe don't throw back thirty Jello shots then drive your Subaru Crosstrek onto a tennis court. People were playing at the time and one of them took away her keys so she couldn't leave. The excuse she gave the judge was that she thought the Jello shots would take thirty minutes to melt in her stomach, and her house was only a twenty minute drive away, so she wasn't purposely driving under the influence. If anything, she was the victim, of misinformation, and who's going to pay for the scratches on her Crosstrek?

Triangles

If I had to learn an instrument, I'd probably choose the triangle. It just doesn't look that difficult to me. It doesn't even have a name. Its name is its shape. I attended an orchestral performance of Vivaldi's *Four Seasons* a few years back and I couldn't help but wonder if the triangle player got paid as much as the oboe and flugelhorn players. You don't really hear about famous triangle players. Or perhaps I'm just not familiar with any because I'm not in the loop. They could be the most highly respected members of an orchestra for all I know.

"I met someone."
"You did? What's his name?"
"Timothy."
"What does he do?"
"He's a professional triangle player with the New York Philharmonic."
"Oh, that's... wait, you don't mean Timothy Roberts, do you? I wept at his clear-toned yet shimmering timbre in Mahler's *Fifth Symphony*."
"Yes, that's him. He's very talented."
"You have to introduce me. I have all his CDs."

The Main Bit

I'm pretty sure my coworker Shannon pooed her pants last week. When I went downstairs to find out where the strong smell of poo was coming from, I saw her driving off with her chair in the back of her hatchback. She explained the next day that the chair had broken and she'd taken it to a 'chair repair place' to get it fixed, but sadly there was nothing they could do and they had to throw it out because 'the main bit' was broken.

Hot Cheese

My family went to a fondue party when I was seven, and while my parents were outside dipping bread in hot cheese, two older boys rolled me up in a floor rug, wedged it in a corner, and left me there for over an hour. I cried the whole time and wet myself. When I was eventually rescued, I asked my parents why they hadn't looked for me, and they said they thought another kid at the party was me because we were both wearing yellow t-shirts. The hosts lent me a dry pair of pants to wear, but they were girls pants, so I spent the rest of the evening sitting in our car angry. I turned on the interior light so my parents could see me glaring.

Arithmophobia

I call bullshit on Arithmophobia. I don't have a problem with phobias in general - it's logical to fear heights or sharks - but a fear of numbers just seems kind of convenient. Particularly around tax time or splitting the bill at a restaurant.

"$43.75 each should cover it."
"Ah, I should have mentioned my arithmophobia."
"Sorry?"
"It's the fear of numbers. It's a real thing and I have it. As such, I'd prefer to pay my share of the bill with a haiku about foxes."
"That doesn't seem fair to everyone else."
"*Eyes glistening*
silent, creeping forward
chicken for dinner."
"That's not a even a proper haiku; haiku has a syllable-based 5-7-5 pattern. That was 4-6-5."
"Please stop."
"I'm going to need $43.75 from you, Gary."
"I feel attacked."

Fish

I don't eat fish because of the smell. I can't even sit next to Holly when she orders fish in a restaurant. I can't sit across from her either, because she'd be breathing at me, so I sit at a different table. Holly and Seb love sushi, so when we go to a Japanese restaurant, it's like they're on a date and I'm just some weird guy sitting at the next table staring at them while sniffing his salad. The salad is the only thing I can eat at sushi restaurants. I do like the vegetarian cucumber rolls, but I won't eat them because the guy who made them touched fish.

Spandexy

More than three years ago, I wore a pair of Holly's underpants because I had run out of clean pairs of my own. I admit to wearing them the next day as well, because they were spandexy, but that's only twice a long time ago. While having dinner with Holly's parents last night, her mother stated, "I was watching a show about Hitler last night and apparently he liked dressing up in women's clothing."
"Really?" Holly replied, "David wears my underpants sometimes."

Short Men

Short men are sneaky. That's why most of them are pickpockets. I saw a movie once called *The Incredible Shrinking Man* in which some guy shrunk down to the size of a pea. There was a scene where he jumped up and down screaming, "Please notice me. I'm down here. For the love of god, please notice me." That's essentially how short men spend every waking hour. It's more of an internal jumping and yelling, but it's there in every nuance and probably a DNA thing passed down from a time they weren't invited on mammoth hunts.

"Can I come?"
"No, you'll just get trampled. Stay here with the women and weave a basket or something."
"I won't get trampled."
"To be honest, it's not your safety that's the issue. The other cavemen find you annoying."
"In what way?"
"Just the whole thing really. Like the way you stick your elbows out when you walk. It looks like you're carrying invisible buckets."
"What about Krog? He likes me."
"No, he doesn't."

Walkers

Our neighbour Janice, a 93-year-old semi-mobile corpse, has a sign in her front yard that says, *Though I may stumble, I will not fall, for the Lord upholds me. Psalms 37:23.* Which is false, as I've seen Janice fall at least three times. Despite a decade of using a walker, it's as though each outing is the first time she's ever seen one; there's no 'lift, place, step, repeat' rhythm, its just random flailing and clanking. I saw her using it upside down once, she was holding onto the tennis balls. On one occasion, she somehow managed to throw the walker twenty feet in front of her, fell, and couldn't get up for several minutes. I would have eventually helped, but a UPS driver stopped and lifted her off the road before I finished my coffee.

Honey

When I was ten, my Uncle Rob jumped from the top of the Rundle Mall car-park after his wife - my Auntie Ruth - declared herself a lesbian and moved in with a woman named Helen who owned a bee-keeping farm. We weren't allowed to have honey in the house after that.

A Bit of a Show

It's unfair that only women get to change their name when they marry. Both the husband and wife should get to do it.

"Okay, you're welcome to go with Williams, but I'm pretty much sold on Starblazer 9000."

It's possible getting a new name is the reason women care more about weddings than men do; it symbolises a new beginning, a new identity. Guys don't get a new identity; they just get the wife and have to be in a lot of photos. It might also be the reason women organise the weddings; they like a bit of a show. Guys would just have a barbecue with a few mates over. Maybe a bit of backyard cricket.

"Congratulations, Barry. Very nice."
"Thanks. I got it at Lowes. 25% off with a coupon. It has a smoker."
"No, I meant the new wife. Where are you going for your honeymoon?"
"I don't know, maybe Six Flags if the weather's nice next weekend."

Office Smokers

It's annoying that you can't smoke in offices anymore. Say what you will about smokers, we don't care, a smoker is far more productive if they're allowed to chain-smoke at their desk. Otherwise, we're just killing time until we feel it's been long enough to go outside and have another cigarette without non-smoking coworkers giving us that look and stating, "You're going outside again?" Yes I'm going outside again, this is what you and your fellow non-smoking cult members have forced me to become; I could have had six weeks work done in the last four hours but instead I've ordered a pair of pants on Amazon and read a Wikipedia article about bamboo.

Jodhpurs

If I were a woman, I'd go for the horse-lady look: ponytail, jodhpurs, tall boots, and a vest. I'd drive my Land Rover into a paddock to look at my horses and my fiancé James would be with me and he'd tell me how great my butt looked in jodhpurs. Then we'd head home and change into our tennis gear.

Wiener Dogs

I could never own a Dachshund because they're also known as wiener dogs. I'm not a fan of the word wiener. It's annoying to say, like the name Gwyneth, and very American, like the words candy and diaper. Americans reading this will probably be thinking, "the fuck else you gonna call candy and diapers, dude?" Which is fine. Y'all do y'all, I just don't want to say the word wiener more often than I have to.

E.Coli

The branding agency I work for shares a building with a business that makes 'edible arrangements'. For those unfamiliar with edible arrangements, they're similar to flower arrangements, but constructed of fruit slices that strangers have touched and breathed on. I was positive the business would be bankrupt within a few months, but apparently there's a demographic who thinks, "I should probably send Helen something for her birthday, but I don't like her enough to send flowers. If only there was something similar but with E.coli..."

Gary's Bottom

Gary hurt his back last week, while demonstrating how butch lesbians walk, so we all had to sit through a thirty minute video about workplace discrimination this morning. It was titled *There's Something Odd About Tony* and, going by the amount of brown, was filmed in the early eighties. Tony gets picked on for being effeminate, and kills himself, and the mean guys get fired. One of them says, "But it was just horseplay!" and a voiceover - which sounded a lot like Kevin Bacon - stated, "Was it though? Was it just horeseplay to Tony?" Also one of the guys rubbed his eyebrows a lot.

"Okay, the video was a bit dated, but the point regarding consequences of workplace discrimination remains relevant. Are there any questions?"
"Was that Kevin Bacon doing the voiceover?"
"I don't think so."
"It sounded like him."
"Are there any questions about the video?"
"Yes, why did we have to watch it with Gary? He's the only one here who's homophobic."
"No I'm not. I don't care what people do with their bottoms as long as they don't touch mine."
"Nobody wants to touch your bottom, Gary."

Show & Tell

A kid at my school once brought in a monkey made out of coconut shells for Show & Tell. His family had visited Bali. It was pretty much the best Show & Tell item ever and I was quite annoyed. I always struggled with my Show & Tell items and had to make things up about them to create interest.

"This is a dinner plate from the Titanic."
"Really David? It looks like a normal everyday plate."
"Yes, but if you lick it, it's salty."

It's not as if my show & tell items were the worst ones though. One of the kids in my class, a girl named Louise, brought a different stick to show each week. There was nothing special about the sticks but she came up with a unique description and use for each.

"This is a brown furry stick. It's 72 centimetres long and looks a bit like a snake. You could use it to stir paint without having to bend over much."
"It's very similar to the last stick you showed us, Louise."
"No, this one is longer."

Copper Wire

A Christian motorcycle club called God's Squad visited my school in third-grade to tell us how cool it is to love Jesus. Two women danced to an Amy Grant song while waving scarves, and a fat guy told us he used to steal copper wire from construction sites until he had a dream about holding hands with Jesus. It pretty much cemented for me the fact that loving Jesus isn't cool.

Tongue Drum

Holly ordered a tiny metal squashed-orange-shaped instrument from Amazon last week. You play notes by hitting it with a toothpick with a bead on the end. Apparently it looked bigger in the photos. It came with a booklet on how to play *Mary Had a Little Lamb*, but Holly prefers to compose her own masterpieces.

"Play the *Bong Bing Bong Bong* tune again, Holly. I find it relaxing. Especially while I'm watching television."
"Right, well I don't want it to play it anymore. Thanks for ruining my dream of becoming a professional tongue drummist. It was number 36 on my bucket list."
"Just skip to 37; owning a fruit stand on a beach."
"That's not 37, 37 is riding an ostrich."

Deck Pics

A guy I sold a treadmill to on Craigslist two years ago sent me a photo of his penis last night. He immediately apologised, explained the message was meant for someone else, and asked me to delete the photo. What makes him think I'd want to keep it?

"How's the deck you're building coming along, David? Do you have any photos?"
"Sure... here's one of the posts going in... that belongs to a guy I sold a treadmill to... and here you can see the first planks going down. We went with a composite for its durability and UV rating."

Albanians

There was an Albanian kid named Amar at my school whose mother had a moustache. It was thick and black and curled up at the ends like a 1940s magician. I once asked Amar why his mother didn't just shave it off, and he spat at me. I'm not a fan of Albanians. That's not racist as I have no idea which race Albanians belong to. An angry and hairy one obviously, but there's quite a few of those.

J.C. Penney

Shopping at J.C. Penney makes me sad. It's dimly lit, the clothes are all polyester, and the staff just stand there staring at you. If you make eye-contact with any of them, they point and hiss, drag you off, and make you go to sleep next to a big pod. Next thing you know, you're working at J.C. Penney. You probably still remember fragments from your previous life, but they're fuzzy disconnected memories; all that matters now is checking if there's a pair of size 9 Muk Luks in the back.

North Star

My partner Holly is a terrible navigator. Her inability to plot and execute any trip is exacerbated by the fact she thinks she's a modern-day Magellan.

"It's your next left."
"Are you sure, Holly?"
"Yes. The North Star is currently 4.8 degrees below the meridian with a slight Equatorial bias."
"That's not the North Star, it's a plane."
"Your next right then."

Small Talk

I'm terrible at small talk. Apparently the key is to show genuine interest, but who has genuine interest on tap? If everyone just agreed to stop making small talk, conversations in general would be a lot shorter and conversations about things you couldn't care less about could be avoided altogether.

"So we took our cat to the vet last week. Turns out the sluggishness was due to her diet. We changed her food to a high protein mix and she perked right up."
"I have no interest in what you are saying and I wish you would go away."
"Righto then. Bye."

Language

I've never been good at learning languages, I can't even be bothered with English half the time. I know most of the commonly used English words, like envelope and rubber, but up until fairly recently I thought the word nonplussed was a math term, and cajole was a type of stew with clams.

Pretty Big Puddles

I flew to Asheville with my coworker Walter recently. Walter doesn't fly much and when the attendant asked the mandatory exit row question about being able to assist with evacuation in case of an emergency, Walter told her he's an excellent swimmer.

'Why would you tell the flight attendant that?"
"In case we crash in the water."
"It's an inland flight, we don't fly over the ocean."
"There's rivers and lakes. And ponds."
"That's true. If we crash in someone's pond, you could swim to the edge and grab a net. What about puddles? Are you an excellent puddle swimmer?"
"I've seen some pretty big puddles."

Dwarves

I'm not a fan of dwarves. It's the way they run mainly, like they don't have bendable knees or elbows. That could be viewed as discriminatory, but dwarves don't care. They don't have feelings like normal humans, it's more of a hive-mind thing, like wasps. Female dwarves lay their eggs in figs.

Pocket Knife People

My partner Holly gave me a pocket knife for my birthday this year. Having one might be handy if you need to cut string or open an Amazon box, but I generally open boxes in our kitchen and there's an assortment of knives in there. I don't recall the last time I needed to cut string. Also, I don't wear the same pants every day and I lack the discipline to remember to transfer a knife to that day's pants. Pocket knife people probably don't own a lot of pants; maybe a pair of Wranglers for work and another 'best' pair of Wranglers for Olive Garden. I've seen photos of Holly's past boyfriends and they all look like two-pants guys. The type who work in a warehouse, maybe driving a forklift. When Holly needed string cut or a box opened, the boyfriend probably said, "I got this, babe." Women like that. It's an ancestral thing from when we lived in caves and knife-based duties were the guy's responsibility.

"Grok, there's a sabre-toothed tiger in the bathroom. I'd stab it myself but if I touch your knife, menstrual spirits will enter the blade and it will have to be thrown off a cliff."
"I got this, babe."

Cruise Ships

Remember that time everyone on a cruise ship got sick and they wouldn't let them off for three weeks? People had to eat mice to survive. My parents went on a cruise once and my mother caught Legionnaires disease from a contaminated spa filter. She had to spend three weeks in hospital so my father sent my sister and I to stay with our Auntie Phyllis who made us sand her floorboards. Also, don't expect the onboard entertainment to be anyone you've heard of. It will be an old guy named Andrew who knows four magic tricks.

热狗

I know a girl named Eileen who had chinese characters tattooed on her wrist that she claimed said 'journey' but turned out to be 'hotdog'. Despite Eileen's protestations that the Google translation was incorrect, it became her nickname, which she was pretty angry about. For someone who liked to portray an air of spiritual superiority and supposedly practiced Buddhism, Hotdog was surprisingly short tempered.

Memories

It would be nice if we could organize memories like files on a computer; deleting the painful or pointless memories and flagging the important ones. I realise *all* memories, useful and horrid, make us who we are, but that's the point; I'd be a better me. One who knows how to do long division and read Morse code. I wouldn't have to work any more, I could just spend the next ten years on *Jeopardy!* and retire a billionaire.

"And we welcome back our returning champion, David. It's his 2690th show and he's playing for ownership of Sony Studios. Good luck, David."
"Luck doesn't come into it. I am knowledge."

Be Best

In 2018, topless model and First Lady of the United States, Melanoma Trump, initiated a public awareness campaign to combat bullying called *Be Best*. Within days of its launch, all bullying, worldwide, ceased to exist. Good job, Melanoma.

Arizona

Our dog Banksy can't just take a dump in one place like a normal dog, he does a weird poo dance for thirty feet while screaming. It's extremely annoying and part of the reason I hate taking him anywhere. Someone always asks if he's okay and I tell them I don't know because he's not my dog, I'm just looking after him for a week while his owner is in Arizona.

Smart Things

My offspring recently changed all our light switches to 'smart' switches. We can't just flick lights on or off anymore, we have to use an app. He also changed the light bulbs for smarter light bulbs, and swapped our door lock for one that whirrs and beeps and sends text messages if you forget your eighteen-character code which has to include a special character. A talking box controls everything now. We're basically living inside a robot that doesn't understand Australian accents.

"Alexa, turn on the television."
"Purging oxygen."
"Cancel that please."
"Setting oven to 450 degrees."

Ashley Furniture

Our senior designer, Jodie, announced this morning that she's now a lesbian. She made the decision after a guy she met on Tinder stole a television and a lamp from her house while she was taking a nap.

"How does someone steal a television *and* a lamp? He must have made two trips."
"I wouldn't know, I was asleep."
"What? Was it a sleepover date?"
"No, it was after lunch. I made chicken enchiladas and then took a nap."
"With him there? Had you met this person before?"
"No."
"So in the middle of a date, at your house, after eating enchiladas, you said, 'I'm going to take a nap.'"
"I just felt really tired all of a sudden."
"Ah. Maybe he drugged you. It could be his modus operandi. Did he molest you?"
"I don't think so."
"It was definitely all about the television and lamp then. Was it a nice lamp?"
"I got it from Ashley Furniture."
"So no then."

Applebee's

Whenever my partner Holly and I go out to dinner with her parents, Holly becomes mute. Her parents rarely have anything to say either, so it's like being with three pod people. Pod people that stare. Once, when I was unhappy about eating at Applebee's, I refused to be the one who broke the silence and we sat staring at each other for 4 minutes and 22 seconds. I timed it on my watch. When the silence *was* finally broken, it was just Holly stating, "David's unhappy about eating at Applebee's."

Last Words

Apparently the most common last words are, "Am I going to die?" - which isn't very quotable. The problem with coming up with quotable last words is you'd have to know that the next thing you say is going to be the last thing you say. If you managed to come up with something good like, "In a world full of choices, choose kindness," then didn't die right away, you'd have to wait awkwardly. Probably looking around at everyone nodding. Nobody wants their last words to be, "No, hang on, I thought of a better one."

Reflective Glass

We have reflective glass in our boardroom window and people regularly check their hair and clothing as they pass by. Sometimes people lean against the window and jump when you bang on the glass. Once, a homeless man took a dump. Our creative director Mike chased him off with a poster tube and our secretary Melissa had to wash the turds down a drain with a hose. The water pressure is pretty low at work so it took her an hour. There was a bit of carrying on and a lot of gagging so we closed the blinds.

Moving

I helped my friend Joseph move recently. After we'd loaded a trailer with boxes of musty clothes, a stained mattress, and a rickety kitchen table, I asked him if we were taking it to his new place or to the dump. Apparently his grandfather had made the kitchen table but I'm not sure how that changes anything. Sorry your grandfather was a shitty carpenter, should we kick the legs off the table before throwing it into the trailer with the rest of the junk or toss it in as is?

Sponge Rules

This morning, while our creative director Mike was pitching a new range of product designs to the CEO of Smucker's, Walter, our junior designer, flung open the boardroom door and asked, "Can you please tell Jodie she's not the boss of sponges?"

Instant Death

I'm always doubtful when I read that someone 'died instantly' in an accident. Nobody dies instantly unless they're vaporised. There has to be a moment where they think 'what the fuck' or 'dear god that hurts' before their brain neurons stop firing.

"If it's any consolation, he died instantly."
"Well that's something I suppose."
"Yes, he convulsed and flailed for two minutes until the brain neurons ceased firing."
"How is that instant?"
"The bit where he died was instant."
"What about the convulsing and flailing bit?"
"That doesn't count. The trick is in the wording; he *died* instantly. Everyone does."

Chevrolet

My neighbour owns a Chevrolet pickup truck with a big sticker across the back window that says Chevrolet. I assume it's so that people driving behind him can tell it's a Chevrolet without having to get close.

"What kind of pickup truck is that in front of us?"
"I'm not sure, I'll speed up and check..."
"Just be careful, the roads are icy."
"Oh, wait, apparently it's a Chevrolet. I don't need to drive dangerously close because he's got a big sticker on the back window that says Chevrolet. We should get one of those stickers for our Hyundai. One that says Hyundai obviously, not Chevrolet."
"Yes, we should. You can't put a price on safety."

Bats

I watched a documentary about bats tonight. I thought I might learn something, but I guess if you've seen one documentary about bats, you've seen them all. There's only so much ground you can cover really; we all know bats can see moths with their ears.

Quick Trips

My partner Holly always asks, "Are you hungry?" two minutes into any trip. It doesn't matter where we're going. When I reply, "No, not really," she says, "Okay," in a way that indicates she's a bit disappointed and was hoping I'd say, "Yes, let's get Qdoba!" for the first time in fourteen years of being asked.

"You're not even slightly hungry?"
"Not at all."
"I could probably eat. Only if you want to though."
"I'm good."
"I'll just eat something later then. I'll be okay. I might wait in the car while you get the potting mix though, I'm feeling a bit light-headed... whoa, I think I just blacked out for a moment. Do you hear bells?"

Playdate

My mother once arranged a playdate for me with a muscular dystrophy kid named Jason. We spent four hours doing a jigsaw puzzle of London's Big Ben. Jason's mother made me promise I'd visit again, but thankfully Jason died.

Gravel

I went on dozens of field trips during my school years, but they were only ever to the local gravel quarry. It was always during summer and at least one kid would collapse from the heat. There's very little shade at gravel quarries. If you've been to a gravel quarry during summer and are thinking, "It wasn't that bad," it just means you've never been to a gravel quarry during an Australian summer. We're talking 50°C in the shade and there isn't any. Also, not a lot changes in gravel quarries; if you've been on one field trip to a gravel quarry, what's the point of going another twenty times? They're not going to discover a new type of gravel.

"And can anyone tell me what this rock is called?"
"Gravel."
"Correct. You have an excellent memory."
'We were just here last week."
"You sure were. And can anyone tell me what kind of rock this one is?"
"A slightly bigger bit of gravel?"
"Correct."
"Are there any other types of rocks here? Apart from various sizes of gravel?"
"No, just gravel. It's a gravel quarry."

Lung Cancer

I've been smoking for forty years, so it's astonishing I haven't got lung cancer yet. I guess it's only a matter of time. There's not going to be any shocked expressions in the doctor's office.

"You have lung cancer, Mr Thorne."
"Oh my lord, how could this possibly happen?"
"You smoked a pack a day for forty years."
"Yes, but I drink a lot of water."
"That doesn't have anything to do with it. Besides, a glass of water every four or five days isn't a lot."
"I also take multi-vitamins, the chewy ones. And I did yoga once."

Ordinances

The village I live in forbids burning rubbish in your backyard because a horse burnt to death in 1876. The fine is a shiny shilling or forfeiture of your least-unattractive daughter to the village elders. There are also ordinances against pitching your neighbor's well and rolling your sleeves above the elbow while churning butter.

Trailers

I don't like towing a trailer. I'm convinced that every time I go over a bump, the trailer hitch is going to jump off its little ball thing. It has to be something that happens, otherwise you wouldn't need the safety chains. I'd almost prefer the chains weren't attached, that way a wayward trailer would be everyone else's problem, not mine. I'm 51% sure the trailer would just be dragged - with a lot of noise and sparks and screaming - until I found somewhere to pull over, but what if there's a pothole? Who even came up with the ball thing to tow things with?

"So it just rests on top of a ball?"
"No, it's held there with a tiny piece of metal."
"Seems a bit dodgy."
"It really is. That's why I added safety chains."
"To keep the hitch off the ground if the trailer comes off the ball?"
"No, to keep it attached to the vehicle while it's shaking violently and nosediving into potholes."
"And you're set on calling them 'safety chains'?"
"Yes, I was going to go with 'life-changing experience chains,' but it's a bit of a mouthful."

Emma

I had a relationship with one of my sister's dolls when I was nine. It was a four-foot tall Snow White doll that I renamed Emma. I didn't have sex with Emma, but I kissed her a lot and told her I loved her. We did almost consummate our relationship one day when my parents took my sister to a soccer match, but the other team forfeited and my parents returned early to discover Emma and I in the bath. I never saw Emma again and I had to have 'the talk' that evening. My mother also borrowed a book from the library titled *What's Happening to Me? An Illustrated Guide to Puberty* and left it in my room with a sticky-note that said, "You're normal."

Last Trip

My friend Bill died a few weeks ago. He didn't have any family so I was given his ashes. Bill once told me he'd like to visit Indonesia one day, so I put the ashes in a padded envelope, stuck ten dollars worth of stamps on it, and mailed it without a return address to the Nandini Resort and Spa in Bali.

Dr Phil

If you're an American visiting Australia and are asked where you're from, the correct response is, "Canada." Though it may be shocking to learn, not everybody thinks Americans are as awesome as you know you are. If you can't bring yourself to pretend you're Canadian for five minutes, then at least try to tone down the whole 'guest on *Dr Phil*' thing. You're probably shaking your head at this point because *you*, personally, are nothing like the guests on *Dr Phil*, but you are. You all are. I don't personally have anything against Americans, I married one, but the fact remains that all Americans can be summed up by three television shows: *Dr Phil*, *The Invicta Watch Hour on QVC*, and *Lip Sync Battle*.

Rope

I only book hotels rooms that have a balcony so I have an escape route. There's an average of 3,800 fires in hotels each year in the United States and I'm not burning to death just because some kid six floors below me decided to stick a fork in an outlet. I used to ask for extra sheets to ensure there were enough to construct a rope ladder from, but now I just pack my own rope.

Dead Coworkers

If you ever need to dispose of a coworker's body, simply drive to a forested area and sit them against a tree with a compass in one hand and a map of a completely different area in the other. If the coworker is known to enjoy hiking, people will say, "At least he died doing what he loved," and if he's not the type to go hiking, it will explain why he was so bad at it.

Away Suitcases

I could never stay in a hostel. They're not for people who own The Bigger Carry-On with built in charger and matching toiletry bag in Coast Blue from Away, they're for people who own saggy backpacks and visit countries like India and Indonesia because they can get a bowl of pingtongpok and a stick-&-poke tattoo there for eight cents.

"How was your trip, Darrell?"
"So spiritual. I bought this bead bracelet for three cents from a child with no legs. I talked him down from five. Can I crash on your couch for a week? You'll hardly notice I'm here, I spend most of my time playing my tongue drum. Do you have any quinoa?"

Animals

My friend Geoffrey can't just sit quietly when we drive anywhere. Silence causes him to break out in a rash so he fills it with gossip, facts about the middle ages, and complaints about traffic light cycles. When he's run out of nonsense to talk about, he creates stupid games.

"Let's play *Animals*."
"Do you name an animal and I use the last letter to name another animal?"
"No, I make an animal sound and you have to guess what it is. I'll go first. Araack!"
"That just sound like someone yelling the name Eric. Is it Eric's mother?"
"No, it's Araack!, not Eric. I'll give you a clue, it's brown."
"That doesn't help much. I give up. What was it?
"Oh don't give up yet. I'll give you another clue. It has long eyelashes."
"Right, well I don't give a fuck what it is, it sounds dreadful."
"It was a seal."
"It didn't sound anything like a seal. Seals bark."
"No, that's dogs. Because you didn't get it, I get to go again. Braaad!"

Design Rule #72

As product packing has never reflected the contents, any disappointment the recipient has upon opening the package is entirely due to their own high expectations and therefore their fault.

"Oh no, the box is full of spiders!"
"And? Your disappointment is entirely due to your own high expectations."
"You told me it was a puppy."

Sleep

I read somewhere that you need less sleep as you get older, but I think it's more of a tick-shaped curve. You're forced to sleep as a child, evade it in your teens, then crave it as an adult. Eventually you have nothing better to do; the staff at the senior living facility have heard all your stories, nobody wants to play Cribbage, and someone stole your teeth.

"Exciting news, Mister Thorne."
"I have a visitor?"
"No, we're having mashed carrots for dinner."
"Okay, definitely wake me up for that."

Vape Oils

I know a guy named Brandon who blends his own vape oils. I don't know him well, but he did invite me to his wedding. I didn't go because it was a *Harry Potter* themed wedding and we had to bring our own wands.

"Try this blend..."
"Okay... hmm... it's very *coconutty*."
"Yes, I used coconut as the base, but can you identify the other flavours?"
"Mint and pomegranate?"
"No, despondency and self-disgust."

Seattle Real Estate

"So it's a cardboard box on the side of a street?"
"Yes, but check out the view."
"How much is it?"
"6K per month but that includes use of the pool."
"There's a pool?"
"Technically it's a puddle, but it's yours to use whenever it rains. Which is quite often. That's why the box has a tarp over it."

Bluetooth

I know a guy named Brian who wears a huge Bluetooth earpiece like you used to see people walking around with in 2003. He calls it his 'receiver', I call it 'Brian's embarrassing Borg thing'. It looks like he has a garage opener attached to the side of his head and it has a green light on it that flashes constantly for no reason - unless it's to warn low-flying aircraft.

"Do you have any peripheral vision, Brian?"
"Not on my right side, no. It needs to stick out that far though, so I can see the flashing light."
"Does the flashing light mean it needs recharging?"
"No, it's just a flashing light. You don't recharge this model; it takes the same 9-volt battery as a smoke detector. Lasts about six months."

Gazebo

Holly's parents bought the world's smallest gazebo last month. I think they got it from Home Depot. There was room for two, but only if you pointed your knees in different directions. Someone stole it last night, so that should give you some idea of how small it was.

Selling Brooms

My friend JM is in a club called the Elk's Lodge and he invited me to a meeting once. I'd assumed it was some kind of vacation timeshare in the mountains and I was going to be offered a few nights free stay in exchange for listening to a short presentation, but it turned out to be a bunch of old men in ill-fitting suits standing in a brown room eating luncheon meats and sharing hip-surgery updates. One of the old men gave me a twenty-minute detailed account of his trip to Target to buy a toaster, and another scolded me for being Australian. Apparently he knew an Australian during the war, possibly the Civil War, who stole his watch while he was sleeping. It was a watch that had been handed down through his family since the Mesozoic period. Not having Bill's side of the story, I suggested the watch may have been lost, and was met with a slammed down plate of luncheon meats and the yelled rebuttal, "It was on a chain!"

I didn't go to any more meetings because JM told me that once a year, members have to go door-to-door selling brooms for deaf kids.

Gary's Pants

My coworker Gary smells like urine. I think it's because once you reach a certain age, your penis waits to be put away after urinating then says, "Hang on, here's a bit more." Also, your sense of smell fades with age, so even if you give your pants a quick sniff and think, "These are good for another day" they're probably not. I used to keep a can of air freshener on my desk and spray it at Gary whenever he approached, but our HR manager made me stop because Gary claimed he had asthma when he was six. There's no rule against pulling my shirt up over my nose whenever he's close though.

Clippers

I cut my own hair. The last time I went to a hairdresser was in 2008 and I ended up with a weird puffy mohawk like the keyboard player in Depeche Mode. I was pretty upset about it and wrote several bad reviews online about the hairdresser. In one of them, I said that I felt like I'd been raped by an escaped lunatic, and the hairdresser replied, "Grow up. I told you not to move while I was using the clippers."

Blobby Wet Cheese

I'm not a fan of blobby wet cheese. I don't care if that makes me a cheese philistine, enjoy your blobby wet cheese, I'll have a bit of Colby Jack if I'm feeling adventurous. I read somewhere that blobby wet cheese only became a thing during the Middle Ages when the inhabitants of a besieged castle ran out of food.

"Barry, try this. It looks like baby vomit but tastes like a blobby wet cheese."
"No thanks. I realise we're besieged and have run out of food, but that doesn't mean we have to resort to eating rancid scraps. Is there anything else?"
"There's still a bit of rat left. Just the head though."
"I'm good."

Gluten

Having access to the company mail server isn't always a good thing. My coworker Lucius once took a photo of his poo and emailed it to his mother stating, "My poo is very yellow." His mother replied with, "Have you been eating a lot of bread? Your tummy might be reacting to the gluten."

Fireworks

The village we live in has a 'fireworks spectacular' for the 4th of July each year. It's held on the 5th, as it's cheaper, and it's not spectacular, but it gives the locals something to do other than polishing their tractors.

"Heading to the fireworks tonight, Cletus? I hear they have five this year. Could just be a rumour though."
"Five? Oh Lordy. We're in for a treat. What time are they setting them off?"
"Between 7pm and 7.03pm."

Showers

My father had strict shower rules when I was young. He'd set a timer for three minutes and barge into the bathroom yelling if anyone went one second over. After he ran off with the lady who did the scheduling at his tennis club, everyone took as long as they wanted in the shower. Since then, my showers have extended to two or three hours. Sometimes I'll eat a pizza then take a nap. I had a beanbag in the shower for a while but the stitching rotted and it burst, so now I use a Coleman camping chair.

Subaru Crosstrek

Melissa, our front desk human, turned 27 today, and her parents bought her a Subaru Crosstrek. I think the most expensive present my parents ever bought me was a clock radio. Coincidentally, Jodie, our senior designer, also owns a Subaru Crosstrek. Hers is orange and a few years older though, with a shopping trolley ding in the passenger side door and a stained headliner from when she didn't see a speed bump while drinking a Starbuck's Frappuccino. Jodie financed her orange Crosstrek and still has three years of payments to make.

"Your parents gave you a Crosstrek for your birthday?"
"Yes."
"Oh wow."
"I know, right? I'm so happy right now."
"Me too. For you."
"It even has personalised plates that say MEL94."
"So it does. I considered getting personalized plates for my Crosstrek but then I decided they're a bit tacky."
"Tacky?"
"Oh, I didn't mean yours are. Just in general. I can't believe we both have the same car."
"Not really, mine's a newer model and has heated leather seats."

Hair In a Can

My father once purchased a can of spray-on hair after seeing it advertised on television. It didn't really look like hair unless you squinted or he darted back and forth, but I'm sure there's been major advances in hair-in-a-can technology since then. Don't let my limited experience with the product put you off trying it.

Diversity

Apparently the agency I work for is far too white, so we're currently seeking a black graphic designer. I'm not sure why it's suddenly become an issue, but it would be far easier to just delete the text on our website about being a equal opportunity employer than put it into practice. It's hard enough finding a decent designer without limiting candidates to a specific color - we've only ever had one black person apply for a design position here and his entire portfolio was just drawings of fish. They were pretty good drawings, but it doesn't show range. Mike, our creative director, told him we'd keep his number on file in case we ever get a canned tuna client.

Hobby Lobby

I'm not sure what the hiring policy is at Hobby Lobby, but I think you just have to love Jesus and own a pair of Sketchers. Everything else you need to know is covered in the employee handbook. Here's an excerpt:

Section 3.4: There's a homosexual in the store!

Do not draw attention to the homosexual, simply follow it to a secluded aisle and administer the Seven Sacred Daggers of Tel Megiddo. Note: A single dagger will kill the host, but to expel the demon, all seven daggers must be used. The Seven Sacred Daggers are located in the employee lunch room on the second shelf to the right of the microwave.

Karaoke

My partner Holly has decided to become a professional karaokalist and recently bought a karaoke machine. It has a fuckzillion watt speaker and laser lights that will take out a retina. It's also portable. This means Holly can take it anywhere. And she does.

"So the funeral is at 1pm, followed by a small gathering at my house."
"Ooh, should I bring my karaoke machine?"

Creative Directors

Branding agencies are only as good as their creative director, and anyone can claim that title. There's no competency test, you just start an agency and write Creative Director on your business card. It's like buying a kayak and proclaiming yourself admiral of the fleet.

"Are you questioning my orders?"
"No, I'm just saying that the left fork of the river opens to a 300-foot waterfall and we'll die."
"How many stripes do I have on my sleeve?"
Sigh "84."
"85, I awarded myself another for adroit paddling."
"Adroit?"
"Yes, it means clever or skillful. I'm both. The trick is to keep the paddle shallow. Hold on, it seems to be getting a little rough ahead. Let's try lying down to lower the centre of gravity."

Disability

I lost sight in my left eye once. It was only for a few minutes after accidently stabbing myself with a drinking straw while driving, but I know what it's like to live with a disability.

Whistle

I chipped a front tooth when I was twelve. It wasn't a huge chip, but for the next few years, whenever I said the letter F, I whistled. It wasn't just a whistly noise, it was like blowing an actual whistle. I couldn't play a tune with it, it was just the one note, so it wasn't like a new skill. I never got it fixed, I just learned to say 'th' instead of 'f' as it was better to have people think I had a lisp than to whistle, then one day I *tried* to whistle and couldn't, so I guess it just sorted itself out.

Letter to Graham's Mum Circa 1982

Dear Mrs Bentley,

I love you. Mr Bentley doesn't love you as much as I do and he has too much hair on his chest. It looks bad. If you divorce him and wait for me to turn 18 I will buy you a car.

Love from David

P.S. Don't tell Graham. P.P.S. Do you love me?

☐ Yes ☐ No ☐ Maybe

P.P.P.S. What is your name? Is it Debra?

Magic

I don't like movies about magic. I don't care if it's magic rings or magic kids, they're all pointless and have the same ending. You may as well just fast-forward to the 'and then he did magic and won' bit because I'm not paying attention.

"Who's that guy? Is he magic as well?"
"That's Bilbo. Have you been watching at all?"
"Oh, he looks different with wet hair."

Goths

Most Goths had admitted by the late 90s that it *was* actually a phase. Robert Smith held on, but have you seen him lately? He looks like Beetlejuice's dad. Fat girl Goths lasted the longest as relinquishing their point of difference meant going back to being normal fat girls.

"Still a Goth I see, Susan."
"Please call me Duskblade. And yes."
"Well I admire your commitment. You're the only Goth I've seen at the mall today. The only one I've seen since 1997 actually. Heading to Hot Topic?"
"No, to the food court."

Philosophy

I don't really have a philosophy, I think it's okay to just wander through life finding interesting things until you die, but if I had to come up with one, *try not to get bitten* works. It covers most aspects and is sensible advice. I suspect most people get their life philosophies from Facebook posts. It should be a rule that you have to come up with your own. My coworker Rebecca has the quote 'Live, laugh, love' above her desk. It's in a rustic frame with a twig glued to the top. You know the kind; Hobby Lobby sells them to pleasantly plump women with dusty homes. They're in the aisle next to the tin roosters.

"Live, laugh, love, Rebecca?"
"Yes, it's my philosophy. That and dance like nobody is watching."
"They're not really yours though, are they? It's not as if you sat in a cave contemplating the meaning of life and decided 'live, laugh, love, and dance with abandon' pretty much covers it."
"I just liked the frame."

Peloton

Holly has been hinting at a Peloton for Christmas this year, but I looked it up and it's 2K plus a monthly subscription. I ordered her a Huffy mountain bike instead - same thing but with fresh air. I also bought her a Rachael Ray nonstick saucepan & skillet set with bonus spatula and egg rings, so someone's getting spoiled.

Landscaping

I ordered a set of 'Japanese Lanterns' from Amazon last week. The description said, "A centuries-old traditional art form, these lanterns are sure to take pride of place in any garden." I received a foot-long string of lights, powered by a single AAA battery, with four tiny plastic lanterns. There were meant to be five, but one of the LEDs was missing a lantern. I doubt Japanese people living centuries ago invited guests out to their garden to show off their foot-long string of plastic lanterns.

"They're beautiful, Mr Yamaha, but is that LED missing a lantern?"
"Yes, I should probably wrap a bit of tape around that LED so it isn't so obvious."

Magnetism

Holly made me go hiking last weekend and we almost died. I've been on maybe three hikes in my life, and I've never claimed to be a hiker, so how would I know how much water you're meant to pack? I drink about a cup per year, so I assumed a 600ml bottle would be plenty. Things were said, some of them quite hurtful, and we took a shortcut back that wasn't.

"We should have bought a compass."
"What good would that do us, Holly?"
"It would show us the way back to the car."
"Do you know how a compass works?"
"I don't need to know how to use one. It works itself through magnetism."
"And what direction is the car in?"
"How the fuck would I know?"
"Then what good would having a compass do?"
"Don't pretend you're a compass expert."
"I know how to make one. You rub a needle on cloth to create static, put the needle on a leaf, and float it in a pool of water. The point of the needle will turn and face north."
"And then you just follow the needle?"
"Yes, until you get to Santa's house."

Heather Locklear Ballerina Disney

My family had a cat named Heather Locklear Ballerina Disney when I was young. My sister was told she could name the cat but there should have been some ground rules. Heather Locklear Ballerina Disney eventually hung herself on a Venetian blind cord and was replaced by Heather Locklear Ballerina Disney 2. After Heather Locklear Ballerina Disney 2 went missing, a rule was implemented about names that aren't too embarrassing to put on lost posters, but it wasn't adhered to; our next cat was named Susan. Susan died when a sheet of metal roofing my father was replacing fell and cut her in half.

Acid-Wash

Acid-wash denim was big during the Eighties but I wasn't a fan. There was just too much happening. The only positive thing that can be said about acid-wash denim is that it hides cum stains well.

"Wow, is that an acid-wash jeans and jacket ensemble?" "No, I'm just completely covered in cum. Accident at the horse wanking farm."

Muscle Twinge

I agreed to do a fun run last month as it was on a work day and I was informed it would be a casual walking thing. It turned out to be an obstacle course and there were people wearing spandex and those stupid wraparound mirrored sunglasses doing stretches and giving each other high fives at the starting line. Two of our five member team left immediately, but Joylene from HR and Kevin from accounts guilt-tripped me into staying. None of us finished. Kevin bowed out when he got a leg cramp within the first few minutes, Joylene fell in mud on a rope swing obstacle, and I was disqualified for taking a cigarette break behind a log. Joylene didn't speak to me for a week, but I dismissed her claims of being pushed as fanciful.

"It was probably just a muscle twinge."
"It wasn't a twinge. I know what a push feels like."
"You wouldn't have made it across the rope swing anyway. Better to go down at the edge than in the middle. Being stuck in the middle would hold up everyone behind you."
"We were last. The only person behind me was you."
"I didn't complete the fun run either."
"No, but you're wearing the t-shirt that says you did."
"I got further than you."

Splash

My father had a thing for Darryl Hanna in the eighties. He took me to the cinema to see *Splash* four times. I also saw *Splash* a few times when it was released on VHS, and several times since on television, so I feel qualified to state that at the end of the movie, when Darryl Hannah and Tom Hanks run to the edge of a pier and Darryl dives into the water, it's one of the worst dives ever captured on film. It's in the trailer if you want to check for yourself, but honestly, it's more of a belly-flop than a dive. You'd think a mermaid would know how to dive properly. I have two theories about why the director didn't say, "Okay, cut, that was the worst dive I've ever seen and you'll have to do it again." The first is that it was a stunt person wearing the only wig and when he or she hit the water, the wig came off and was lost. The second is that the stunt person died.

Parenting

Praise is an integral part of parenting, but if you're taught that you're a ten when you're really a four, it creates an inflated notion of importance. That's why I randomly tell my offspring Seb he's 'not all that'.

Hacky Sacks

Hacky sacks were popular for one week when I was at school. Nobody cared about them until the day Sarah Hutchkins put one in a sock, swung it around her head, and belted Miranda Reynolds in the face during gym. Everyone had hacky sack socks after that. The teachers thought it was a new game until factions formed and the red socks attacked the blue socks during assembly one afternoon. Two kids had to be taken to hospital. Hacky sack socks were banned after that and were replaced by drink bottles filled with piss. It meant long lines at water fountains and bathrooms during recess, but a few entrepreneurial kids sold sandwich bags of piss for ten cents if you were low on ammunition.

Thyroid

Fat people always claim they have a thyroid problem. It may be true, but it's also easy to blame something that can't defend itself.

"I have a thyroid problem."
"Oh fuck off, Jodie, don't blame me. You ate fifteen pancakes at iHop this morning. I'm doing the best I can under difficult circumstances."

Mange

My offspring Seb has been growing a beard and I'm not impressed. It's as if one moment he was a fresh-faced teenager, and the next, a filthy old peasant from the middle-ages. The kind that peers a lot and wears one of those leather hats.

"Ist thou a beggar or an alley-rapist?"
"Neither m'lord, simply a humble peasant making his way to the kitchen to microwave a Hot Pocket."
"Be thee on your journey then, I wish not to gaze upon such wretched facial hair a second longer."
"'Tis the fashion m'lord."

Gardens

Holly and I visited The Japanese Friendship Garden in Phoenix recently. It wasn't that impressive; if you've seen one carved rock pagoda you've seen them all, and we have koi at home. Holly had some notion about walking the path together, but I could see her head above the foliage whenever she crossed arched bridges from my bench. I waved the first couple of times but she didn't wave back so I didn't bother after that.

Dave Matthews

People who wear beanies like Dave Matthews. They listen to it while vaping in their friend Steve's bedroom, nodding along as they flick through mountain biking magazines and discuss the best spoke tightening tools.

Parent-Teacher Nights

I hated parent-teacher nights at school. They mostly consisted of my parents nodding sadly while I stared at the floor. Once, my teacher asked if I'd been tested for autism. I had no idea what the term meant and thought she was implying I might be some kind of child genius.

"If I pass the test, can I can skip the rest of school?"
"What? Be quiet, David. Have you been listening to anything your teacher has said?"
"Yes, I was going to take it home but she made me put it on the wall with tape."
"What are you talking about?"
"My painting. The one of a frog."
"Nobody mentioned a painting. We were discussing the fact that you need to pay more attention in class."
"The corners rip when you use tape."

Fire Pits

I always avoid the fire pit when I'm staying at a resort or hotel that has one. It doesn't matter if there's nobody else sitting at the fire pit, if you sit down, other people will show up. When they do, you can't just get up and leave, you have to wait it out a bit so it doesn't look like you're only leaving because they sat down. Once, when Holly and I were in Colorado, a guy with a guitar sat down next to us and started playing *Wonder Wall*. I asked him to leave and he said, "You don't own the fire pit."

Pizza

If I could only ever eat one food for the rest of my life, I'd pick pizza. It's whatever the fuck you want with bread.

"No, you have to pick one kind of pizza."
"You're not the hypothetical food police. Fine, I'll have an 'everything' pizza and pick off the stuff I don't feel like eating that day. Just pile it up with mangoes, spaghetti, cheesecake, soup etc. Maybe chips and dip."
"I'd pick sushi."
"Of course you would."

Movies About Feet

I read an article about Daniel Day-Lewis recently which said that during the filming of *My Left Foot*, he stayed in character for his portrayal of a wheelchair-bound person with Cerebral Palsy for the entire shoot. Crew members had to feed and carry him over cables, to and from set, and help him use the bathroom. If I were one of the crewmembers and my boss said, "I'm going to need you to wipe Daniel's arse because he's pretending he can't do it himself," I would have resigned immediately. I haven't seen *My Left Foot*, because I don't watch movies about feet, but from what I can tell it's about a guy who can move his left foot. I can move both of my feet and nobody has approached me about the movie rights.

"So, David, we received your script titled *My Left and Right Foot and My Legs and Both My Arms and Hands*, but we're a little confused by the plot. It's about a man who has full working use of all his limbs?"
"That's right. He's perfectly fine."
"Okay. Does he have any special abilities or talents?"
"No, not really. He can draw a little bit."
"Oh, portraits and the like?"
"No, just cats. They're not very good though."

Hit Men

I've often thought it would be handy to know people who know people that kill people. The people I know only know people who can get kitchen faucets at cost or have a used chiminea to sell, and it's too late for me to start hanging out with the wrong crowd now. I've seen people in their forties wearing leather jackets and it's sad. Besides, if I did know people who know people that kill people for money, I'd probably get carried away and people would be dropping like flies.

"David, the client doesn't like the layout. Can you get a revised proof to him by Wednesday?"
"No need."

Marketing

I've never been a fan of promoting my own books. When I have to, I feel like one of those old guys you see holding Little Caesar's Pizza signs on main roads.

"And what do you want to be when you grow up?"
"A pole."

Factions

When I was ten, our school principal committed suicide by jumping off the roof of the administration building. It happened on a Sunday, and the area was cleaned before Monday morning, but a girl in my class named Louise was convinced that the top of an acorn she found was actually a bit of the principal's brain. Even after it was proven not to be a bit of brain, Louise refused to acknowledge it. Several other acorn tops of various shapes and size were shown to her, but she'd just say, "That's a different colour," or "That doesn't have as many wiggly bits." It was very annoying. What's worse is her friends backed her up and claimed that the bit of brain Louise discovered was soft and pink. It wasn't soft or pink, it was hard and brown, I'd seen it. Factions formed between those who believed it was a bit of brain and those who *knew* it was the top of an acorn. Imaginary lines were drawn in the playground and brainers weren't allowed to play with acorn toppers. Guards were posted at the slippery dip ladder and you had to show an acorn top to gain access; acorn toppers kept an acorn top on them at all times. This went on for nearly a month until a boy named Jason handed out birthday party invites and Louise admitted it may have been an acorn top so she'd get one.

Agitation

Every five years or so, I think, "A bath might be nice," but after sitting in it for five minutes, I remember why I don't take baths. It's like sitting in a really small pool; you're in water but you can't do laps or lay on a floatie, so you just stare at your knees. My partner Holly likes baths as she finds them relaxing. Her baths aren't relaxing for me though as I'm responsible for pre-bath preparation. This includes scrubbing the bath, drawing the bath, adding bubble-bath, and agitating the water. I did it once for her, because I was feeling guilty about something, and now it's expected. Like back rubs. There's nothing worse than getting into bed, making yourself all comfy, and hearing, "Will you rub my back?" I usually pretend my arms are too sore from all the bathtub scrubbing and water agitation.

Kayak

I know a guy named Nigel who once catfished his sister Tanya on a dating site by pretending to be a helicopter pilot named Jake. Tanya sent him several nude photos, including one with a Sharpie in her anus, and Nigel used them to blackmail her into buying him a kayak.

Christmas Rug

Holly goes all out decorating for Christmas. Our house looks like Santa's cave in a department store. I quite like the stockings on the mantel and the red bow on the front door, but I hate the Christmas rug.

"It's not a Christmas rug, it's a tree skirt."
"What's it for?"
"To hide the tree stand. You don't like it?"
"It's not the kind of rug we'd usually have in the living room."
"We don't usually have a fucking tree in the living room either. What's your problem with it?"
"It's just a bit, I don't know, Goodwilly."
"Goodwilly?"
"Yes, like it came from a Goodwill store. It's the fabric I think. And the pattern. And the size and shape."
"Right, sorry for trying to make it festive around here. Maybe we should take down all the decorations. I don't even want to have Christmas anymore. Thanks for ruining Christmas, Uncle Scrooge."
"The billionaire duck?"
"No, the grumpy old man that made Tiny Tim sell matches on Christmas Eve. You really need to read the classics."

Dustpan Dustpan

My father thought highly of his own wit and probably felt he deserved some kind of comedy award for coming up with alternative names to the bands my sister and I listened to in the eighties. Kiss became Piss, Duran Duran became Dustpan Dustpan, and Adam and the Ants became Spasm In My Pants. My sister and I once attempted to create a list of alternative names for the artists he listened to, but nothing rhymes with Demis Roussos.

"What about Demis Kangaroussos."
"Hmm, it's a bit weak but I'll add it to the list. What other records are there?"
"Leo Sayer, Captain & Tennille, the Bee Gees..."
"Bee Gees rhymes with Wee Wees."
"Okay, that's actually brilliant. Write that one down."

Thoughts & Prayers

"I'd like to redeem these thoughts and prayers, please."
"Sure, how many do you have?"
"Sixteen. My wife is fairly active on Facebook and our youngest has leukemia."
"Nice. You can get a Breville toaster for that."

Girls Named Louise

I went to school with a girl named Louise. She had tight curly hair and a moustache. Once during a game of soccer, she ran to the edge of the field, dropped her shorts, and did a poo. This is the kind of thing people named Louise do. The gym teacher had to pick it up with a plastic shopping bag.

Impressions

I don't like to brag, but I think I could win *America's Got Talent* with my impression of my coworker Gary. I'd need a decent sob story of course, as that's the only way to get to the finals.

"So, tell us about yourself, David."
"I was born without arms or legs and my parents burned to death in a forest fire when I was five. Also, I have cancer and tapeworm."
"And what are you going to be doing for us today?"
"My impression of Gary."
"Okay, let's see it."
"Help, I've fallen and I can't get up."
"Well, that's a yes from me."

Breakups

When someone breaks up with their partner, it's best to simply say, "I understand you being upset, she/he had many defining qualities," and follow it up by nodding. Nobody will ask, "Like what?" even if they want to, so after nodding for a bit, you can go back to doing whatever it is you'd rather be doing than talking about feelings. You're not meant to say anything bad about the person they've broken up with, because when they inevitably get back together, it will be held against you.

"How's it going with you and your girlfriend?"
'We went through a rough patch and broke up..."
"You dodged a bullet. She had a face like a smashed crab and I heard she once sucked off a dog."
"Then we worked through our issues and got back together. She's just gone to the bathroom and will be back in a minute."

New Orleans

I'd rather be dead than live in New Orleans. There's only so much jazz I can handle and it's none.

Balloon Animals

I'm not a fan of clowns. I don't know anyone who is so I'm not sure why they're still a thing. People must have been easily entertained in the olden days and probably thought five clowns getting out of a small car was the height of comedy. They probably talked about it the next day around the water cooler at the Bakelite factory like people in the nineties did about that episode of *Friends* where Phoebe sang a song about a cat. I went to a classmate's birthday party when I was six and there was a clown there making balloon animals and hats. I asked the clown for a balloon hat and he made me a sausage dog. When I complained that it wasn't what I'd asked for, he grabbed my arm really fast, squeezed hard enough to hurt, and said, "I don't give a fuck what you want kid, take the fucking sausage dog."

I intended to tell an adult but when I approached the classmate's mother, the clown appeared out of nowhere, grinned menacingly at me, and asked loudly, "Do you like your sausage dog?" and I replied, "Yes, thank you."

I realize it's not much of a clown story but it's my clown story. It was a long time ago but if I knew who that clown was and he was still working, I'd leave a bad review on Yelp. I think his name was Barry.

Dollar General

Most people have cable these days, so the market for aerials that sit on the top of your television has to be small. You can still buy them at Dollar General stores though. Some of them have a little plastic satellite dish on them to trick people into thinking they'll get transmissions from space.

"Look Evelyn, this television aerial has a little satellite dish on it. We should get that."
"We already have a television aerial."
"Yes, but ours doesn't have a satellite dish."
"What do we need a satellite dish for?"
"HBO."

Crimper

My sister bought a hair crimper in the early eighties. It was a popular product at the time. The first time she used it, she left it on too long and fried her fringe off. There was still some hair, but it was only about a centimetre long and really spiky. I wasn't allowed to comment or stare at it, which was pretty difficult.

Robots

I thought we'd have proper robots by now. I bought an iRobot to do my vacuuming, but what they don't show you in the commercials is all the banging into furniture and beeping when it gets stuck. It takes about two hours to clean a small room and I'd rather suck the dust up with a straw than listen to the horrible thing whirring around banging and beeping for two hours. If I leave the house with it running, it manages to clean about four square inches before getting stuck. Once I found it upside down and another time it disappeared for a week when I left the back door open.

My coworker Mike bought the lawnmower version of an iRobot last year. He used it once then packed it away after Duncan, his Yorkshire Terrier, attacked the mower while it was operating and lost a paw. Not all of the paw, just the pad and toes, but Duncan has a weird nub now that makes me feel ill when I look at it.

"Look who's come to visit the office. It's Duncan! Yes it is! Say hello to David, Duncan. Can you shake hands?"
"It's fine, really, he doesn't need to do that."

Exercise

If I had to describe my body type, I'd say its melancholy and crepes. I should exercise, as I'm not getting any younger, but it seems like a lot of effort. There's no way I'm performing a squat on purpose and I'd do anything to avoid a plank. I remember seeing a product advertised on television years ago which just zapped you fit. You attached a couple of sticky metal electrodes to your stomach and it gave you muscles while you watched television. I'd probably give that a go. It's not cheating if the end result is the same.

"I need to lose twenty pounds."
"Okay, you have three options. You can inject yourself with diabetes medicine, jog, or be zapped."
"How many times would I have to jog? Like more than once?"

Anne Frank

I haven't read *The Diary of Anne Frank*. I'm sure it's a fine book, and hats off to Anne for inventing Braille, but I honestly couldn't care less about a deaf girl hiding in a wardrobe.

Gravy

Complaining about dinner when I was young would result in a loss of television privileges for the night. Which may not seem harsh, but my father's version included a chair next to the television that you had to sit in and watch the rest of the family watching television from. If you turned your head towards the television, he'd yell, "Pause." Three 'pauses' and you were 'off' which meant sitting in the chair with a tea towel over your head.

"Wow, you're certainly missing an exciting episode tonight, David. It isn't a holiday resort planet after all, it's a trap set by the Cylons. Starbuck and Apollo are walking straight into it. Perhaps you'll think about that the next time you decide to comment on how lumpy the gravy is."

Snake Bite

My mother was bitten by a snake once. It wasn't venomous but we didn't know that. She must have seen an episode of *The Lone Ranger* or something because she asked my father to suck out the poison and he replied, "No point in both of us being poisoned."

Magic Trick

When I was twelve, a kid named Wayne Redding tried to convince me to stick a golf ball up my bum by showing me how easy it is if you use margarine. When I refused to participate, he attempted to choke me. The next day at school, he told me he was only joking and hadn't really put a golf ball in his bum, it was a magic trick.

Bumps

My father enjoyed camping when I was young. I didn't. While he sat in a camp chair sipping beer, it was my job to clear a flat area to pitch the tent on. I had my own shovel and pickaxe.

"My arms are getting tired."
"Keep going. There's still bumps. You know how the Egyptians got their land level for building on?"
"How?"
"They flooded the area with water. Whatever stuck out of the water, they'd dig away."
"You want me to pour water on it?"
"No, don't be stupid. Why would we pitch a tent in mud?"

Television

I know a couple, who aren't homeless, that don't own a television. Not even one in their bathroom. I won't visit them as it means having to look at each other and come up with things to say. Things other than, "Why don't you have a television?"

Hentai

I discovered Hentai porn on a coworker's computer last week. One of the videos was about a woman with both male and female genitalia. There was a flashback to when she was a famous pop singer, then she had sex with a rock monster while floating in space. When they climaxed, there were a lot of flashes and a planet exploded. Back on earth, a lady holding a small boy's hand pointed up at a bright light in the night sky, presumably from the exploded planet even though light doesn't travel that fast, and the boy did an excited running on the spot dance and shouted, "Naya nomble can!" It was pretty bad but who am I to judge? I've closed browser windows and sat silently thinking, 'What's wrong with me?' many times. The last time was after watching a Youtube video on how to build your own swimming pool out of railway ties.

Amazon Reviews

Someone once gave one of my books a one star review because their copy was stolen from their porch. I'm fine with people giving me one star if they think a book I wrote was crap, most of them are, but how is it my fault if a package is stolen? Buy a Ring doorbell if you live in a shitty neighbourhood. Your package will still get stolen but you can post the video on the Ring app and an old lady named Janet will leave a comment about people having no respect for other people's property since they stopped teaching the Bible in schools.

Magnets

We have so many fridge magnets, birds regularly crash into our windows. Half of the magnets aren't even from places Holly and I have visited; they're places Holly's parents visited and brought back for us. Why would I care that they went to the M&M factory in Tennessee? We also had a plastic alphabet on our fridge, but my offspring Seb kept writing 'David is gay' with the letters so I threw them out. I did attempt to write 'Seb is gay' but I dropped the letter S and it went under the fridge. Whatever goes under the fridge belongs to the fridge.

Physical

My friend Dominic bought the album *Physical* by Olivia Newton John when it came out. It had a poster inside, of Olivia in leggings and leg warmers, and where the crotch was meant to be, there was a hole.

"It came that way."
"But it's all wet."
"Just fold it up and put it back in the cover."

Omega 3

Holly recently read that Omega 3 aids brain function, and is now convinced she's like the blackboard guy in *Good Will Hunting*.

"Test me. I ate a can of StarKist tuna for lunch."
"Okay. What's 1296 divided by 18?"
"184."
"That's not even close."
"I was fast though. I'd be like Rain Man if I was good at math. We should go to a casino."
"So you can count cards quickly but incorrectly?"
"No, for the buffet."
"I don't understand the connection."
"That's because you don't eat fish."

Piercings

I know a guy named Roger who got his bottom lip pierced because my friend Bill told him he looked like the lead singer from Blink 182. When Roger showed us afterwards, Bill said, "Oh, I meant the lead singer from Phish." Roger's lip became infected and, despite a course of antibiotics, turned into what looked like mango puree. Eventually he had to have a chunk removed and the two sections of bottom lip sewn together. The reduced width pulled the top lips in at the sides and now he permanently looks like he is about to say something.

"And, if you look at the next slide, you'll see we have... yes Roger?"
"What? I didn't say anything."
"Sorry, I thought you were about t... yes Roger?"

Grapes

My birthday parties as a child weren't popular. One year, my father came up with game called *Whoever sands the most paint off a dresser wins a bag of grapes.*

Dry Balls

My partner Holly makes me go to her parent's house for Thanksgiving dinner each year - which is practically domestic abuse. The only thing vaguely edible is the dry balls; bread dipped in milk, rolled into a ball, and baked. I usually only have one dry ball because it takes thirty minutes to swallow. After dinner, we sit in the living room watching The Weather Channel for four hours in silence. Occasionally someone comments on how good the dry balls were, but conversation is kept to a minimum as Holly's father Tom, who is going deaf, makes a big production of turning the volume down every time someone speaks, then turning it back up to its highest setting when they've finished.

"The dry balls were good this year, Tom"
"What?"
"The dry balls."
"Hang on," ▮▮▮▮▫▫▫ "What?"
"I was just saying the dry balls were good this year. Best dry balls I've ever had in fact."
"What about the dry balls?"
"They were good."
"Maria, what did David say?"
"He said the dry balls were good."
"Oh." ▫▫▫▮▮▮▮

Dumpster

Mike, our creative director, threw our spiral binder in the dumpster this morning. Melissa had to climb in to retrieve it; it's one of her job roles. Throwing things into the dumpster is Mike's way of dramatically expressing annoyance at them, but it's become so commonplace that Melissa keeps a stepladder and a robot claw, the kind that old people use to reach jars on high shelves, behind the dumpster.

"Fuck this laptop, it's going in the dumpster."
"Melissa is away today."
"First thing tomorrow then. Remind me."

Trophies

I've only ever won two trophies. One was third place in a Spelling Bee when I was nine, and the other was second place for 'longest streamer' in a kite-decorating contest. My kite design should have come first, but they gave that to a Down syndrome kid who glued a peacock feather onto a Batman kite.

Trust British Paints?

My friend Geoffrey once told me that James William Miller, an Australian serial killer responsible for the rape and murder of seventeen women, was his second cousin. Apparently Geoffrey met him once, at a family get-together when Geoffrey was five, and James showed Geoffrey how to make an origami frog.

"It's hardly a claim to fame, Geoffrey."
"Wow, jealous much? Sorry you're not related to anyone famous."
"Rolf Harris is my uncle."
"The wobbleboard guy? What a joke."
"He's more famous than your murdering second cousin. Rolf Harris was in the British Paint's commercial. He tapped on a can of paint and said, 'Trust British Paints? Sure can.' Everyone knows the slogan."
"It's weak. It's not even a slogan. It's just a question with a 'yes'. Trust socks? Sure, why not? Trust that cat over there? Probably."
"It's better than 'Let's bury the bodies at the Wingfield Dump.'"
"Not by much."

Excel

Our department has to take part in Excel training next week, and Joylene (who has four framed photos of her cats and one of her dead father holding a trout on her desk) stated, "Ooo, I love Excel." Who says, "Ooo, I love Excel."? How is it a sentence? If there ever comes a time where I'm excited about using Excel, it will be time to turn off my computer, pack my stuff, and start a fire. Along with photos of cats and dead fishermen on her desk, Joylene has a vast collection of scented candles with names like Highland Bog, so it will be easy to make it look like it was her fault.

Self Checkout

I'm not a fan of the self checkout. I just want to hand over my stuff and a card and have someone else do the work. I wouldn't use the self checkout at all if it wasn't for the fact I can get $100 worth of groceries for $12 by scanning a bag of dried red kidney beans twelve times.

"Can I check your receipt please, sir?"
"No, I left my baby in the car."

Adult Diapers

My Auntie Brenda came to live with us when I was eight. It wasn't convenient for anyone and I had to hug her once. I'm not sure what her illness was but she lost her hair and coughed a lot. Often she'd cough until she soiled herself and there was a special basket in our laundry for her bedding with an airtight lid. Sometimes my sister would remove the basket lid and lock me in the laundry. Once, she threw a used adult diaper at me and urine went in my mouth. I've not mentioned the incident since as I'm waiting for the right moment.

"David, the doctors have given me less than two weeks to live if I don't find a donor kidney. I know it's a big ask but, as my brother, I was wondering…"
"Remember that time you threw a used diaper at me?"
"What?"
"Urine went in my mouth. Auntie Brenda's urine."
"Okay…"
"It was very upsetting at the time. I thought it meant I had whatever she had. I wrote a will. Something to think about as your dialysis machine fails and you convulse to death."

Maps

My father once drove six hundred miles in the wrong direction during a family trip across Australia and blamed my mother for folding the roadmap wrong.

"You have to fold it in the middle, then over, then across twice... no wait... then over again, then across twice."
"What does it matter?"
"The creases go the wrong way if you don't fold it properly."
"Why don't you just admit you missed the turnoff?"
"It was in a crease. Facing the wrong way."

Shark Tank

"So it's a baseball cap with a small hole cut in the brim?"
"That's right. It's a cap toothbrush holder."
'What if people need more than one toothbrush while they're out?"
"It comes in one, two, and three hole models."
"What are your sales?"

Costumes

Our production manager, Rebecca, sews outfits for her cat. I'm not sure why, I guess she was just sitting around one day and thought, "Fuck this shit, I'm forty and single, time Jack had a Peter Pan costume."

"And here's a close up of his felt hat."
"Right, but what's it for?"
"He's Peter Pan!"
"Yes, I can see that, but why?"
"Because it's adorable!"
"Okay."
"And here's one of him sleeping."

I've seen photos of Jack dressed as a pirate, a fireman, a cowboy, a fish, and Edward Cullen without feeling anything. Not even pity for the cat. It's one of those fluffy ones with the pushed in face, the kind that stares at you with disgust as if to say, "Who invited you to Endor?" I'm not a fan of any type of cat but if I'm watching a news report about one being rescued from a burning building and it turns out to be the fluffy pushed in face kind, I'm particularly disappointed.

Moonraker

My fifth grade teacher, Mrs Bowman, died while our class was watching *Murder on the Orient Express*. We thought she was asleep so we ejected the video and watched *Moonraker* instead. There was talk of changing the name of the school library from The Hansard Library to The Edith Bowman Library, but the Hansard family wasn't happy about it, so they named the cafeteria after her instead. They put up a sign, and a framed photo of Mrs Bowman eating a sandwich, and Mr Bowman attended the ribbon cutting. He looked bewildered by the whole thing but posed for a photo behind the counter serving a student a sausage roll.

Couple's Costumes

Holly takes Halloween seriously. She starts planning her costume the day after Halloween as it takes 364 days to perfect. One year, she dressed as Neytiri from the movie *Avatar*, and had to start putting on her costume a week before Halloween as it included prosthetics and an animatronic tail. As Holly likes us to have couple's costumes, I was a tree.

Springs

Two of my coworkers, Ashley and Walter, have been dating for several months, and are currently having a deep and meaningful in the courtyard at work. I can hear everything they're saying if I stick my head out of my office window: it's not eavesdropping if you already know the topic, it's secret participation. Apparently Ashley threw cheese at Walter during an argument over a brochure layout, and he's rather upset about it. It was a triangular block of parmesan - not a soft cheese like mozzarella - and it could have really hurt if he hadn't ducked in time.

"It's just lucky I have reflexes like a taut spring."
"Springs don't have reflexes, Walter."
"Taut ones do."
"No, they don't."
"What about the spiral ones in watches?"
"They're taut but they don't have reflexes."
"Fine. Reflexes like something quick then. Have you seen that video of a mouse quickly jumping away from a snake?"
"No."
"I'll send you the YouTube link."

Crabs

I watched a documentary about crabs last night. I learned a few things, but I don't foresee any future conversation where that knowledge will be useful.

"Crabs are decapods, meaning they have ten legs, and can reach speeds of up to 20mph."
"What's that got to do with catching a cab?"
"I thought you said catch a crab."

Lottery Winners

I saw an interview a while back with a guy who won the lottery. When the reporter asked, "How will this change your life?", the guy replied, "It won't really, I'm still going to go to work Monday morning." Please. The only logical reason to go to work Monday morning would be to see everyone's expression when you arrive by solid gold helicopter.

"Well I'm off, just dropped by to say it's been horrible and I hate you all. Have fun being poor."
"Um, we're going to need two weeks notice, Bob."

Gentle Ben

I wasn't a fan of the television show *Gentle Ben* when I was young. It was just *Flipper* with a bear, and in every episode the bear saved the day by tugging a rope. It wouldn't matter what the issue was, a bank robbery or bomb diffusion, the bear tugged a rope. A kid, who was friends with the bear, would then make a rope related pun such as, "Guess they got roped into that one," and the kid's father would laugh and tussle the boy's hair. Apart from coming up with a different rope related pun each week, working on the script must have been a cushy job.

"Right, episode 82, there's a cattle stampede and the bear tugs a rope and saves the day."
"Right, but why are cattle stampeding in a marsh and how would tugging a rope stop them?"
"You're overthinking, Greg, just work on the rope pun."
"Fine. How about, 'well he sure roped them in'?"
"Didn't we use that in the episode where the bear saved the school bus from going over a cliff?"
"No, that was, 'Ropey ropey rope rope'."
"Ah yes, not one of your best."

That's How You Get Nits

I caught head lice at school once. There were products available that killed lice, but my father just shaved my head. We didn't own clippers, he used shaving cream and a razor. I wasn't the only kid at school with a shaved head though, there'd been a bit of a pandemic and apparently other parents had also been too embarrassed to go to a pharmacy.

"Do we have to shave it all off?"
"Yes, I'm not walking into a pharmacy and buying a bottle of Nonits just because you decided to rub your head on some other kid's head."
"I didn't rub my head on anyone's head."
"Well you must have, that's how you get nits."

Bunkers

When I was about eight, my class watched a movie called *The Day After*, about a nuclear attack. Afterwards, our teacher had us write an assignment about who we'd let into our bunker and why. Most of the class wrote that they would include their parents, siblings and pets. I chose Jeannie from *I Dream of Jeannie*.

Teenage Pregnancy

A girl at my school named Vicky had a baby when she was thirteen. It was a big deal at the time because most of us hadn't even fingered a girl yet. She named the baby Tom, after Johnny Depp's character on *21 Jump Street*, and it became a fixture at the school. This was before schools had daycare facilities, so I guess her only options were to leave school or take Tom to class. Tom was pretty quiet and Vicky constantly forgot about him. Once he sat in his stroller in the middle of a soccer field for three hours, and another time he was left on a bus.

Pictionary

I've never been overly adept at drawing. It might be assumed that some degree of artistic skill is required to work in the design industry, but there's a vast difference between pencil on paper and pixels on screen. I can split paths and know the names of far too many typefaces, but I'd be the last person I'd pick as a partner on Pictionary night.

"Is it a person rollerskating during a tornado?"
"No, it's a grape."

One Upping

Our production manager, Rebecca, always has to one-up everyone. Once, when I told her I couldn't wrap tape around a box because I had a cut on my finger, she told me she ran the Boston Marathon with two broken legs.

"Sorry I'm late, Rebecca. I didn't get to bed until 2am."
"I didn't get to bed until 8.59am and I still managed to make it here by 9am."
"That doesn't seem possible but okay. You do live closer though. I had to drive here in heavy traffic."
"I had to walk. In shoes made out of crushed glass and thumbtacks."
"That's highly unlikely, why would anyone do that?"
"And it was snowing."
"It's summer."
"Also, a bear attacked me. It tore off both my arms."
"I can see you have arms, Rebecca."
"I guess I just have more respect for other people's time."

Adele

A thousand times? That's stalking, Adele. Time to move on. Sorry, but he's obviously just not into big girls.

Shoplifting

I shoplifted a lot when I was young. I considered going pro but I was eventually caught and my photo was put up in the front window of Target. I didn't shoplift again, the humiliation was too much. I was crying in the photo and lots of kids from my school saw it - it was taken with a flash so my tears were really shiny. In my defence, the guy who caught me took me into a back room, made me strip to my underpants, and ordered me to pull them tight so he could see if there was anything hidden in them. I'm pretty sure that would be grounds for a lawsuit these days. He also took a couple of photos of me in my underpants before he took the one of my face, so who knows what happened to those. They could be on the dark web somewhere - maybe in a .zip file titled *Young Teen Shoplifter in Battlestar Galactica Underpants*.

Gums

Our production manager Rebecca has four-inch gums. Seeing her smile is like watching a documentary about scary fish that live in the darkest depths of the ocean. I'd rather be punched than see her having a good time.

Office Procedures

I implemented a new office procedure last week. At 4.30pm each day, we verbally attack each other for fifteen minutes, then spend fifteen minutes apologising for what was said. This way, everyone leaves happy with all issues sorted. Nobody wanted to participate. Two formal complaints were made and Jodie locked herself in the bathroom and cried.

Bit Rude

I'm no action hero. I've been punched before and it's something I'd rather avoid. I haven't had my mettle truly tested of course, I'd like to think I'd protect Holly or Seb if they were in danger, but there's a chance I'd be that guy who pushes everyone aside in their effort to get away. I threw Seb at an angry chicken once. My highest tested level of protecting those in need is when people are rude to a cashier. I won't say anything to the person being rude, but after they've left I might say to the cashier, "Wow, he was a bit rude." There's no superhero costume for that. Nobody in peril is yelling, "Help me Wow He Was a Bit Rude Man!"

Golf Balls

Golf balls are a lot bouncier than you think. I threw one at a brick wall once, and it came straight back and hit me in the temple. I must have blacked out because the next thing I knew, an old lady was squirting me with water from a drinking bottle. It was in a park and I was 34. My offspring, Seb, had seen the old lady walking her dog and yelled to her for help. I didn't know that though, I just woke up to some old lady squirting water at me so I kicked her.

Coins

My sister Leith swallowed twelve dollars in coins when she was eight. She was fine but she had to stay overnight in the hospital for observation. It was the third time she'd been admitted for swallowing coins. Nobody knew why she kept doing it. I asked her about it years later, and she said that she just liked the taste. Apparently she sucked the coins until they had no flavour left and then swallowed them so they didn't get mixed up with the unsucked coins.

Bag Beans

A coworker caught me stealing coffee beans from the office kitchen recently. I claimed I was putting the beans in a ziplock bag to keep them fresh, but they weren't buying it, so I've had to do it every day since to prove my innocence. It's become a thing; people sip their coffee and ask, "Mmm. Are these bag beans?"

Travel Cupboard

My partner Holly has a travel cupboard. It contains hundreds of tiny versions of products like bodywash, deodorant, and toothpaste, but also tiny plastic bottles and tiny bags to put the tiny bottles in. It has six drawers that are organised to match the human body - hair products at the top, then face, torso, groin, legs, and feet - and if you place anything in the wrong drawer or use an item, Holly knows about it.

"A cotton bud is missing from the travel cupboard."
"And?"
"We've spoken about this. It's fine if you use items, you just have to remember to email me a list of any items you use so I can add them to my travel cupboard Excel document."

Paddleboards

I'm not sure what the point of Paddleboarding is. It's the same skillset as standing on a wobbly stool and nobody's calling that a sport. The person who invented it, probably someone who wears a lot of Prana, should have been told to stop fucking about and sit down.

"Stop fucking about and sit down. You'll hurt yourself."
"No I won't, I have really good balance."
"Nobody cares. What's the point?"
"The point is that I'm standing up. Look at me!"
"You don't look very stable."
"I'm not."
"Or comfortable."
"No."
"You'd be better off in a kayak. They have a lower center of gravity and a paddle with blades on both ends so you can row faster."
"It's not about speed. It's about standing up. I'm going to call it the Stand Up and Paddleboard."
"So it's just a water version of your other inventions, the Stand Up and Drivecar and the Stand Up and Sleepbed?"
"Yes, but I have good feeling about this one."
"That's what you said about the Stand Up and Defecatetoilet and the Stand Up and Rollwheelchair."

M.A.S.H.

I missed the final episode of *M.A.S.H.* when I was eleven because I was sent to my room for poking a hole in the bottom of our swimming pool with a homemade spear. It was the most watched television series finale in history and holds the record to this day. I was seriously bitter about it at the time and brought it up constantly.

"Can you pass the butter please, David?"
"No, because you wouldn't let me watch *Goodbye, Farewell and Amen*."
"That was two years ago, let it fucking go. The war ended and everyone went home."
"I'm sure there was more to it than that."

Body Language

I watched a show on body language recently. An 'expert' analysed a police interview and determined the suspect had lied because he touched his ear.

"Ah, did you catch that? That's a dead giveaway he's either lying or has an itchy ear."
"Oh my god, it's like a special power. Quick, tell me what colour I'm thinking of."

Fence

We had a fence installed at our house recently. I wanted a twenty-foot fence, because I shouldn't have to see our neighbour's shitty yard from our nice yard, but I was informed six-feet is the maximum height allowed by law, because police officers have to be able to climb over it.

"Okay cadets, today's test is to see if you can climb over a six-foot fence. Dennis, you're up."
"Are we allowed to use a ladder?"
"Do you have a ladder, Dennis?"
"Yes."
"Well that's fine then. Greg, hold the ladder for Dennis."
"Couldn't we just go through the gate?"
"Sorry, Greg?"
"There's a gate. We could just go through that. It would save mucking about with the ladder."
"Right, I hope everyone is paying attention because Greg just suggested using the gate. Well done, Greg, police officering isn't just about climbing fences, it's also about improvisation."

Runaway

I ran away from home when I was five. I didn't like it there and knew of a much better house where lots of kids lived - a couple of them were my age. I wasn't sure of the address, but I knew what the front of the house looked like; I'd seen it dozens of times. There was a seesaw in the backyard and the family did fun activities together, like sack racing. I knew there was a spare bed for me in Peter and Bobby's room, because Greg had recently moved into the attic.

Swiffers

Having experienced my coworker Jodie's choice of music during a drive to a client meeting this morning, I finally understand the appeal of Taylor Swift's music; it's the audio equivalent of a caramel Frappuccino. Jodie disagreed with this analysis and stated that if Taylor Swift were a drink, she'd be an expensive champagne, like "Don Pentagon." I commandeered the stereo on the drive back, but a speaker blew halfway through *Banana Brain* and Jodie yelled at me because she's only had her Hyundai Tucson for three weeks.

Ruse

My coworker Gary owns 28 guns. It seems a lot to me, but I'm not American so I don't know what the average is. I like to imagine he has a secret button that makes a wall slide open to reveal shelves of automatic weapons, maybe some grenades, but apparently he keeps most in a safe and the others hidden around the house.

"You have guns hidden around your house?"
"Of course. I'm not going to be the victim if someone breaks into my home to rob me."
"Where are they hidden? Is one taped under your desk like in the movies?"
"I'm not telling you where they are."
"You have one taped under your desk, don't you?"
"No, they're hidden far more strategically than that. My desk is upstairs."
"You could offer to write the robber a cheque."
"Or, and this is just one example, I could act like I'm having chest pain and need my heart pills."
"You're going to put on a play for the burglar?"
"Not a play, a ruse."
"And you have a gun hidden in your medicine cabinet?"
"No, the pills are in a kitchen cupboard. Next to a box of Pop-Tarts."

School Notes

I was a skinny child and extremely self concious about it. I avoided any environment where I would have to take my shirt off in public, such as the beach or swimming pools, and I forged dozens of notes to get out of showering in gym at school.

"David, this note states you have smallpox."
"Yes. Just on my chest though, that's why I can't take my shirt off."
"Smallpox was eradicated over fifty years ago."
"It's a different type of smallpox. Smallerpox."
"Last week you had rabies."
"Yes, a bat bit my chest."

Cement

I concreted a patio last week and, when I realized how many bags of cement I had to mix, I started adding other stuff to fill the forms quicker. There's a piece of rebar in there, but there's also a shoe, two tennis rackets, a sewing machine, a box of computer cables, a fold-up camping chair, and a bag of carrots.

Immigration

When I applied for United States residency earlier this year, Holly and I were interrogated in separate rooms to see if we were really a couple. Most of the questions were relatively easy to answer, but who the fuck knows their partner's birth date?

"It's one of the warmer months. Maybe August."
"Okay. And what side of the bed does Holly sleep on?"
"From which direction? Looking out, Holly is on my left, but if you were standing at the foot of the bed looking at us, I'd be on your left."
"No, you do it like a car. From where you're sitting."
"Right, that makes sense."
"I'll just mark it down as left. Next question. Describe your bed linen."
"Wrinkly."

I think you're meant to take sheets out of the dryer as soon as it stops spinning but who does that? It's like leaving the dishwasher and washing machine doors open when you're not using them so they don't get smelly. Who's walking around their house as if everything is perfectly normal with appliance doors open?

Philadelphia

Most cities have their good and bad points, but there's no point to Philadelphia. From its corrugated roads to its unbearable residents, the entire city is a dump. The only good thing to ever come out of Philadelphia is the cream cheese... No, wait, according to Wikipedia, Philadelphia Cream Cheese isn't from Philadelphia; it was invented in New York in 1872 and got its name as part of a marketing strategy to associate the product with dairy farming, for which Philadelphia was known at the time. Philadelphia isn't known for dairy farming anymore; it's known for meat with cheese on it. How is that a thing? Anyone can stick cheese on meat. Burgers have cheese on them. What else does Philadelphia have to offer? A cracked bell? Who gives a fuck.

Interracial Couples

My friend Joseph is officially dating a black girl he met on Tinder last month. She smokes cigarettes so they have a lot in common. The relationship has meant a lot of changes. Not for him, for everyone else. We're not allowed to make racist jokes anymore, not even ones about bicycles, and we can't sing along to rap songs.

Lag

Zoom meetings are generally painful, but when Gary, our account manager, is included, they're unbearable. He lives in a shed in the woods somewhere and has Dish internet, which only works when there's no clouds. When it is working, his video stream looks like a 8-bit .gif closeup of a Rubik's cube, and the lag is like communicating with someone in space.

"And that's why..."
"And that's why what, Gary?
"..."
"Okay, Gary seems to be hav..."
"...we can't quote for client work that is additional..."
"Sure, but th..."
"...to the original quote. Sorry, did you say something..."
"No, I thou..."
"...while I was talking? I missed..."
"No, go on."
"...it."
"Okay, does anyone else have anything to discu..."
"Over."

Coma

When a kid in my third-grade class died after being in a coma for several weeks, my mother stated, "It may be a terrible thing to say, but it's probably a relief for his parents." Which I took to mean she'd be fine with turning off my life support on the first day.

"So I just flick this switch?"
"Yes, but there's a chance he might come out of it."
"Not much point waiting around though, is there? I'm sure everyone has better things to do. It's not like he was good at math or sports."

Spiral Binder

Nobody likes using the office spiral binder. Yesterday I discovered Walter, our junior designer, sitting in a corner sobbing after attempting to use it.

"I just don't get it."
"It's not that difficult, Walter. You punch the holes..."
"No, I mean about my mom."
"Look, I'm sorry your mother committed suicide but it's been two days and this report on kitty-litter brand recognition isn't going to spiral bind itself."

Yellow

My family didn't have brand name ice creams in the freezer when I was young, we had plastic tubes of coloured ice that you had to snip the top off with scissors. They were better if you whacked them against the edge of a countertop to mush up the ice before cutting open, but not by much. I think they came in packs of 600. There were branded versions available with flavours like Raspberry Blast and Cosmic Blue, but we had the generic brand with flavours like Yellow.

Bezels

I upgraded my iPhone to a newer iPhone today. It's identical to my old iPhone but has a slightly thinner bezel. It's like looking into the future.

"How long have I been frozen?"
"5000 years. Welcome to the year 7021."
"Oh my god. I bet so much has changed."
"Yes, you may want to sit down for this... telephone bezels are 3% thinner. Also bears evolved. They live on the moon now. It's theirs. There was a war."

Air Freshener

My father quit smoking the day he turned thirty. It wasn't willpower, he paid to be hypnotised into believing cigarette smoke smelled like rancid meat. It took surprisingly well; he had to catch a taxi home from the session because of the dirty ashtray in his car. He had the car detailed, and whenever we went on family drives, he made my mother - who smoked well into her fifties - shower and change clothes before she was allowed in. He also kept a can of air freshener in the centre console and sprayed it around occasionally while driving. Once, he sprayed her hair.

Dancing

I can't dance. I've tried on several occasions and fully accept the fact that I look like a marionette walking up stairs while holding two lit candles. People have declared, "Of course you can dance, David, you're just being self-conscious, stop worrying about what anyone else thinks and simply move your body to the beat." But then if I do, they say, "Okay, perhaps you should stop. Are all of your other motor-skills intact? Can you drive a car with a manual gearbox?"

Again?

My coworker Ben's mother died last week. It was lung cancer this time. Last time it was throat cancer; she had to speak through her neck hole using a kazoo. I was surprised when Ben told me his mother had died as I thought she was already dead. That's the thing with cancer, if you get it and then get better and then get it again, everyone's a bit over it by then. Not in a mean way, more of a 'Oh, we're doing this again?' way. If you're related, it's a lot of effort, and if you're not, it's annoying to have to hear about it.

"The cancer is back."
"Again? What's this, like the fifteenth time?"
"No, it's just the second time actually."
"Really? I guess I just assumed from all the complaining that it was more. Must be hard for everyone."
"Yes, it came as quite a shock."
"No, I meant the complaining."

Pride Month

Our village holds an annual Pride march each year, but it's not a popular event. Usually it's just a handful of people waving rainbow flags while dodging beer cans thrown from passing pickup trucks. Someone caught a beer can last year and it made the local paper. The headline was '*Local shares beer with lesbian*'.

The Ashes

When I was eight, our next-door neighbour shot himself in the head. Apparently he'd discovered his wife was having an affair, but I only learned that many years later. At the time, I was told the neighbour had shot himself because the Australian cricket team lost the Ashes to England. It was probably the best way my father could come up with to describe a despondency so bad you wanted to die. He really liked cricket and wasn't big on subtlety. Once, when he and my mother decided to have a trial separation and I asked why, he told me that marriage is like a game of cricket, but without an umpire and with only two players, and one is a bitch.

Bongo Song

We moved recently and our new neighbours are a dwarf and his blurry wife. He might not actually be a dwarf - it's possible he's just very short with weird chubby limbs - and his wife isn't really blurry, just so nondescript that ten seconds after seeing her, I forget what she looks like. I think she has brown hair. Also, her name might be Cathy. Or Jill. I don't care. Apparently they're artists but I've known artists who are capable of using a weed whacker - it's not just about wearing black and bringing rusty dump benches home to put on your front lawn. They don't have blinds, so at night we get the full experience of what it would be like to live in a third-world country. At some point, one of them must have declared, "You know what would make great living room furniture? A beige plastic outdoor setting. And I'll paint it without primer." To which the other no doubt answered, "It will go perfectly with the six-foot papier-mâché giraffe we found in a dumpster behind Pier-1." Also, I once saw the blurry wife dancing in a poncho while the dwarf played bongos. It must have been a bongo song about birds because she was flapping her poncho like wings. It's easy to be judgmental though. Really easy. I'd probably still bother if it took effort though, I'd have nothing to talk about otherwise.

Plank Partner

I had a classmate in third-grade named Oliver who had a metal plate in his head. Apparently he was clipped by a pole after sticking his head out of a bus window, but I'm not sure if that really happened or we were just told that to stop us doing it. There was no point asking Oliver as he only knew three words; tree, mum, and biscuit. Our school wasn't wheelchair accessible, ramps weren't in the budget, so someone had to follow Oliver around with two planks of wood. I was Plank Partner for a whole week once just for farting in class. The school did eventually have ramps installed, but Oliver died before the concrete set so he never got to use them. Nobody else at the school was in a wheelchair so it was a big expense for nothing. To cover the cost, school fees went up, and whenever my father had to pay for a field trip, he'd state, "Ten dollars to visit a gravel quarry? Fuck that biscuit kid."

March

The key to a healthy relationship is discovering things you both hate. That way there's plenty to bitch about other than each other's faults, like March.

Winfield Blue

My parents smoked when I was young. They smoked Winfield Blue because Paul Hogan told them to. They smoked in the house, they smoked while playing tennis, and they smoked in the car. Sometimes when we went on family trips, I could barely see out of the windows.

"Why are you coughing?"
"It's smoky in here. Can I wind down my window?"
"No, the air conditioner is on. I don't know what you're carrying on about, your mother and I are the ones smoking and we're not coughing."
"Just a little bit? I can't breathe."
"Fine. Just half an inch though. You can stick a drinking straw through the gap and breath through that if you are going to be a dickhead about it."
"How long before we get there?"
"Six or seven hours. It depends on the traffic."

Cats

I'm not a fan of cats. It's their their bum holes mostly. I don't want something walking around my house showing its bum hole the whole time. If I had a cat, I'd make it wear pants.

Autism

My parents had me tested for Autism when I was ten. There wasn't any real basis for it, but being on the spectrum would have provided an explanation for my behaviour other than environment. As such, I'd obviously lied on the test.

"I didn't lie. There wasn't even a test, he just asked me questions and showed me photos."
"Photos of what?"
"People's faces. I had to say if they were happy or sad."
"What questions did he ask?"
"Stuff about an old lady leaving money on a park bench and a boy falling off his bike."
"What else?"
"Stuff about school and home and you."
"Us? What did he ask about us?"
"Just if you fight a lot."
"And what did you tell him?"
"That you fight a lot."
"Did you tell him about the time you laid naked on the floor in the bathroom and cracked an egg onto your penis?"
"No."
"Well there you go."

Covered Trailers

I saw a show on television recently called *Tiny House Hunters*. It was about poor people buying trailers to live in. None of them said, "I'm poor and I'm going to live a trailer" of course, they justified their decision by claiming environmental responsibility, or the desire not to be part of the mortgage rat-race, or a love of being able to hitch up their house and travel wherever they want. None of them travelled anywhere though, they parked their 'tiny house' on their parent's property, which their parents must be delighted about.

"You've bought a house? I'm so proud of you. I was wondering when you were going to make your way out into the world on your own. You're forty-five and your job at the glue factory pays well."
"Yes, as of this morning, I'm officially a home owner. It's a lot of responsibility but I feel I'm ready to take it on."
"Well, let me know if you need help moving."
"That won't be necessary, there isn't room for any of my stuff in the new house so I'm going to leave it all here."
"What if you need something?"
"I'll walk across and get it. I'm parking my house in the backyard. Do we have a spare extension cable?"

Banter

Ryan Reynolds and Blake Lively seem like a happy couple. I hate them both, and their children. Name one good movie Ryan Reynolds has ever been in apart from *Deadpool*? And what does Blake Lively do? Is she a country singer? I'm basing their happiness on the public image they've created of course, the witty banter and cute digs, they might be different in private.

"Oh, my banter gets a bit grating after a while does it? That's what I do, Blake. What do you do? Are you a country singer? What songs have you done?"

Guest Bags

When I was nine, my father threw out our threadbare couch and replaced it with four bean bags. Later, he bought another two for guests. The original four were green, but Target had run out of green bean bags when he went back to get more, so the guest bean bags were orange. It made them easy to tell apart and when my sister or I sat on them, my father would yell, "Get off the guest bags."

Helmets

I've never been white-water rafting. Hurtling down a river in a blowup boat with the type of people who give high-fives and say 'Woo!' is on my reverse bucket-list of things to avoid along with marathons and musical theatre.

"Let's spend the day risking being thrown onto rocks and drowning. We get to wear helmets."
"Awesome, what kind of helmets?"
"I'm not sure, I think they're like bicycle helmets."
"Sign me up then, that's my favourite type of helmet.

Ducks?

To get out of bed by 6am, my partner Holly sets alarms for 5am, 5.10am, 5.20am, 5.30am, 5.40am... Each has a unique sound, including marimba drums, a truck backing up, and Harry Styles saying, "It's time to wake up my lovely." I have one alarm, of ducks quacking, and I set it for the exact time I need to get up. It wakes me immediately as I think, 'Ducks? You can't sleep next to a pond, David, you'll roll over and fall in.'

Checkouts

There should be partitions at supermarket checkouts so the people behind you can't stare at your groceries as they make their way along the conveyor belt. It's like they're analysing your meal plan for the week and judging you for all the bread. I usually make a little fort using packs of toilet paper and paper towels to block the view of smaller items, but you have to put the bread on last or it will end up at the bottom of a bag of cans.

Therapy

I've experienced social anxiety, in various degrees, all my life. Sometimes I won't leave the house for months. Apparently one method to overcome social anxiety is to join an 'active behavioural therapy group' which entails sitting in a circle talking about yourself. It's a 'face your fears' approach and the kind of thing I'd pay not to do.

"Oh, you're scared of spiders? Me too. You should join the active behavioural therapy group I'm a part of."
"Will it fix my phobia?"
"No, we just sit in a circle and throw spiders at each other. Big hairy ones. It's dreadful."

Wranglers

I tried growing my own vegetables once, after watching a program called *Preppers* in which people with beards and Wrangler jeans anticipate social collapse. I paid around $30 for seeds, $100 for railway ties, and $250 for fifty bags of garden soil - which means the two cucumbers I ended up with cost $190 each. They weren't even good cucumbers. One was about two inches in length and the other had a huge grub living inside it. Should the grid ever 'go down', I estimate my chances of long-term survival as slim at best. I'll probably be shot at the supermarket and have my cans of evaporated milk and instant coffee taken from me on the first day.

England

I've been to England and I'm not a fan. Everyone's miserable and damp. Also, there's nothing to eat; English people just eat the same three meals their entire lives. It's like all exploration of taste and texture ceased once they discovered mashed potatoes.

Oil Changes

I don't do my own oil changes. I don't even know where the oil stick thing is on my car. My father used to do his own work on our family car, and sometimes I'd help, but I was more of a flashlight holder than an actual helper, and replaceable with a piece of duct tape.

"Why are you shaking the light? Hold it steady."
"I am."
"No you're not. It's like a disco in here. Shine it on the alternator."
"Here?"
"Does that look like a fucking alternator to you?"
"Here?"
"That's the battery. Just hand me the duct tape and go play with your Spirograph or something."

My father had very little patience, so it's surprising I have so much. Once, after getting shocked while fixing a toaster, he placed the toaster in our driveway, backed over it with the car, then threw it like a frisbee over our back fence. It hit the neighbour's six-year-old daughter while she was standing on a pool ladder.

Man Cave

My father turned our garage into a man cave when I was nine. He put a bar, television, dart board, and two beanbags in there. For a while, he had a poster of Kelly LeBrock sitting on a moped in a bikini, but my mother ripped it down during an argument about having her sewing table and chair in the man cave.

"Why can't it be the 'family cave'?"
"We already have a family cave, it's called the living room. This is my area to get away from everyone."
"Perhaps I'd like my own area to get away from everyone as well."
"You already have one."
"Where?"
"The kitchen."
"..."
"You're welcome to visit though."

The following weekend, while my mother was grocery shopping, my father cleaned out our tool shed, ran an extension cord from the house, and put her sewing table and chair in there. After being led outside in a blindfold for the reveal, my mother locked herself in the bathroom and cried.

Some Kind of History

Sometimes when my partner Holly posts a photo on Facebook and a guy leaves a comment, I'll ask Holly who the guy is and she usually answers with something like, "He's the assistant rep for a company that does subcontract work for the company that prints our flyers," so it's probably really someone Holly dated before she met me. Why would anyone write, "Looks great!" about a photo of our new deck unless there was some kind of history there? Keep it in your pants, Todd McNamara.

Adulting

Holly and I bought a proper cutlery set recently. Our existing cutlery looks more like what you'd see on an Etsy wind chime than in a kitchen drawer. Several spoons have taken disposal unit rides over the years and half the knives have made their way into the garage to live as flathead screwdrivers. I don't recall ever buying cutlery before I met Holly. I definitely had cutlery, but it was a random assortment stolen from restaurants. We went with the Fantasia flatware range by Mepra. It was pretty expensive but Holly had Kohl's Cash.

Marooned

If I were marooned on a deserted island like Tom Hanks in *Lost*, I'd want my partner Holly with me as she always has plenty of water with her. She drinks about eighteen gallons a day and is one of those people who puts stickers on her Hydro Flasks. You know the type; well hydrated and a bit overly proud about it. Oh, you drink your body weight in water every ten minutes? Good for you, we're not all part fish. I drank almost an entire 600ml bottle of water two months ago so I'm good for the rest of the year.

I'm one of those people who has watched enough survival shows to think I'd have a two-story hut built on the island by the second night, maybe with a pulley system and a flying fox, but in reality I'd probably be dead within a week. It would be a week of complaining about not having coffee or cigarettes and Holly would thankful when I took my last breath.

"It's okay, you can go. It's time."
"I'm actually feeling a bit better. I might try some of the fish you caught."
"No, that's my fish."

Secrets

When my mother died, my sister kept it a secret from me because she didn't want to share the proceeds from the sale of her house. It didn't bother me too much; she needs the money more than I do. It can't be easy raising five kids from five different fathers who are either in prison or gave false names and addresses and can't be located.

"Who's my dad?"
"Lamp Couch Hallway. He had brown hair."
"Will I ever meet him?"
"No, he's an astronaut and lives on the moon."

Greenpeace

I dated an environmental activist once. At least I thought we were dating. We spent 14 hours chained to a tree in a housing development before she informed me she was a lesbian. It's not easy getting a refund for Greenpeace membership. I had to dispute the credit card charge. I did get to keep the T-shirt though. Really, I deserved it for everything I'd done for the environment. There was a lot of sap on that tree.

The Really Big Pumpkin

Holly's parents, Tom and Maria, visited Gatlinburg recently, and apparently they saw a really big pumpkin. If you ever visit Gatlinburg, you needn't bother with the standard tourist attractions like Dollywood or the Aerial Tramway, because it's the really big pumpkin that creates real memories. I've heard the really big pumpkin story at least fifty times, and, with each retelling, the really big pumpkin gets bigger.

"It was way bigger than a beachball. I couldn't reach my arms all the way around it. I wish I'd taken a photo."

"Have you seen those red balls outside of Target stores? The pumpkin was twice the size of one of those."

"It was as big as a three-person tent."

"I climbed it. There was a ladder."

"If you carved it out, a family of four could live inside quite comfortably."

"It took three months and four days to circumnavigate. Half our expedition died."

"The sun? Pfft."

Farmers

You can't trust farmers. Once, when our class went on an excursion to a dairy farm, a farmer told me cows communicate to each other telepathically and I believed it for several years. I mean, why would a farmer make that up? Sorry your job is so boring you have to lie to an eight-year-old, but perhaps you should consider the repercussions of when they're fourteen and arguing with a biology teacher because they were given false information by a professional in the milk industry.

Rumours

When I was ten, a kid at my school named Michael told everyone I wanked off my dog. For the next three years, kids asked if I really wanked off my dog. I heard several different versions, one had me kissing my dog while I wanked him off, and another had me wanking him off into a cup. I have no idea why Michael said I wanked off my dog. A year earlier I'd told him about another kid, named Jason, who rubbed his dog's penis to prove how big it could get, but I didn't participate in the act, I just said, "Eww, it looks like a maraca."

Elderly Clients

It's pointless arguing with elderly clients. They're not interested in your opinions because they've already discussed theirs with Carol in the lunchroom and Carol agreed with them. You're incorporating 18 point type, 43 colours including Christmas tree green, and a logo visible from space. Boards and councils make the worst clients because they're a gaggle of geriatrics who turn the simplest of issues into seventeen meetings so they can look like problem solvers. It's all they have. That and their 1974 hairstyles.

"And next on the agenda is the ant situation in the kitchen. Any suggestions?"
"If we pour fifty bottles of maple syrup on the floor, the ants might gorge themselves to death."
"Excellent. Take the lead on that project and have a report ready for the next meeting. Something with graphs and maybe clipart of ants."
"I could make the graphs out of ants."
"Clipart ants or real ants?"
"I'll try both."

Germans Telling Jokes

"Hans, I have a very funny joke for you."
"Proceed, Fritz."
"How many Dutch does it take to change a lightbulb?"
"It is not a complicated task so my guess is one."
"Incorrect. The answer is none. The Dutch do not own houses with electricity because they are poor."
"That is a very funny joke. I dislike the Dutch."
"Yes, they drive their camping buses incredibly slow along our Autobahn during the summer holidays, thus causing us to brake our BMW's hard."

Fondue Parties

"Fantastic fondue guys, what kind of cheese is this?"
"Kraft."
"Delicious. Also, I love this album. Boney M are going to be the next Beatles. You mark my words. Have you heard the track, *Ra Ra Rasputin*?"
"Yes, fantastic isn't it? It's just called *Rasputin* though."
"Is it?"
"Yes. They sing 'Ra Ra Rasputin' but the song is just called *Rasputin*."
"Well there you go. I did not know that."

Iwa-Baransu

I was once commissioned to design a brochure titled *Living with Anxiety* which included a list of relaxation methods. Along with the usual breathing and physical exercise suggestions, it described a Japanese technique called *Iwa-Baransu* which requires you to visualise balancing stones to form a stack against a wind. The wind's strength is determined by the issue at hand. Apparently it was a technique practiced by Samurai before battle and now more commonly before business meetings. I tried it prior to a meeting with the client to discuss responsibility for ten thousand copies of the brochure being printed and sent out with 'We'll bring highkicks' listed under services offered instead of 'Wellbeing checkups', but it didn't work for me.

Welding

I read somewhere that if you are watching someone weld and you smell toast, it's the back of your eyeballs cooking. If you're making toast while watching someone weld, this information would, of course, be useless.

Texting

I've never understood why people text while driving. My partner Holly texts me while she's driving all the time, and when I criticise her for it, she declares, "I'm capable of doing more than one thing at a time." Which is true of most people and no doubt a viable justification in court if you're in an accident.

"If I understand this correctly, Mrs Thorne, you were chopping carrots, reading a book, and changing your pants when you drove through the school crossing and killed twelve children. Do you have anything to say in your defence?"
"I'm capable of doing more than one thing at a time."
"Yes, most people are. Excellent point. Case dismissed."

I won't even answer calls while I'm driving.

"I called your phone thirty-four times and you didn't answer. What if I was locked in the trunk of someone's car?"
"Were you locked in the trunk of someone's car, Holly?"
"No, but I can't find the Scotch tape and I need to attach a feather to the end of a pen. Did you put it somewhere?"

Big Mug

Our HR manager signed the office up for a 5K walk for Alzheimer's awareness last month. Her father suffers from it so we all had to pretend to care. Melissa, our front desk human, was assigned the task of ordering team t-shirts for us to wear, but apparently the website was confusing and she ordered coffee mugs instead. I made a point of taking mine on the walk, holding it up as if to say 'cheers' each time Melissa looked my way, but it got old surprisingly quickly and the mug was annoying to carry, so I left it in someone's letter box. I like to think the person who checked their mail that afternoon was delighted. It was a big mug so perhaps they use it to eat soup out of.

"Margaret, have you seen my big mug? The one I got in the mail?"
"It's in the dishwasher."
"Oh no, I was going to have some soup."
"We have soup bowls."
"Yes, but I didn't want a whole bowl of soup, just a big mug of soup."
"What about the stoneware pottery mugs? They're pretty big."
"No, they're too gritty. I'll just go without."

Cloning

People claim they'd like a clone of themselves, but if the technology existed, nobody would do it. Your expenses would double and the conversations would be dreadful.

"Have you seen that movie where the..."
"Yes."
"Just making conversation."
"I'm fine with silence while we moisturise each other. Your voice is kind of annoying. God, is that what my back looks like? It's like a giant chicken breast with moles."

Home Projects

Holly has a formula for any projects I undertake. It's called the 4/6 formula; if I estimate a project will take 2 weeks and cost 2K, applying the 4/6 formula means it will take 4 times as long and cost 6 times as much. It's pretty much spot on every time. We save a lot by not getting permits though. We're taking out a wall next week. I tapped on it and it doesn't sound load-bearing.

Pan Clangers

My partner Holly is a pan clanger. You can always tell when Holly is angry, and the level of anger, by the amount and volume of pan clanging. Once, after I admitted a girl on *Love Island* was reasonably attractive, two pan handles were bent and a pot was dented. I think the longest Holly and I have stayed angry at each other was a week, which is a lot of pan clanging to put up with. I don't recall what that argument started over, but it was one of those full-blown, gloves off arguments where you list their faults in alphabetical order and repeat things they say in a voice that is meant to sound like someone with Down syndrome.

Two or three days is a reasonable timeframe for things to bounce back to normal after an argument. I read somewhere that you should never go to bed angry, but that would mean talking about the argument after you've just had it, which is really just a continuation of the argument. Give it time, sleep on it, do something vaguely considerate the next day to show you're the better person. It doesn't need to be a big gesture like changing the sheets, you can just hand them a teaspoon or something.

Leather Pants

Duran Duran was the first band I ever saw in concert. I was eleven. The ticket cost $13.50 and my cousin Neil took me. I wore a green Slazenger headband and Neil wore leather pants. After the concert, I sat in the front of his Datsun 280B while he had sex in the back with a girl dressed as Madonna. After the grunting and slapping finished, they shared a weird smelling cigarette with the windows rolled up while we listened to *Rio*. A few years later, I received a box of hand-me-down clothes from Neil and the leather pants were in there. I wore them to school once, but they were squeaky and hot and almost impossible to ride my bike in.

Mr Steve

You rarely hear about hamster's dying peacefully in their sleep. My offspring Seb had a hamster, named Mr Steve, which I sucked up a vacuum hose while cleaning Seb's bedroom. I heard a *thok*, but thought it was a sock, and tried to clear the blockage by ramming a broom handle down the hose. I put Mr Steve back in his cage for Seb to find, and suggested dysentery, due to the state of his room, as the most likely cause of death.

Chairs

I hate it when people invite me to a barbecue and tell me to bring a chair. I'm not taking a chair anywhere. I'll stay at home with my vast selection of things to sit on if you can't get your act together.

"I'm having a barbecue tomorrow. Bring a chair."
"Are you having the barbecue in a field?"
"No, it's at my house but apparently I don't own any chairs. Oh, and bring something to drink and a side dish. Maybe potato salad."
"Will anything actually be provided?"
"The venue and great company."
"Right, I'll probably just stay home then."
"No, you have to come. I need you to pick up six bags of ice and a full propane bottle on the way. And a patio umbrella from Home Depot, it's going to be sunny.

I specifically tell people not to bring their own chairs when I have a barbecue. I paid a lot for my outdoor setting and I don't want anyone's shitty Coleman camping chairs ruining the layout. Not enough chairs? Stand. No, we're not bringing the dining room chairs outside, they're West Elm.

Salt-Water Crocodiles

The beaches in Queensland look nice, but you can't go swimming because they're full of salt-water crocodiles. I read about a woman whose poodle was taken by a salt-water crocodile. They were several feet from the shoreline but the crocodile exploded out of the water and closed the distance in a fraction of a second. To her credit, the woman refused to let go of the leash even after the poodle was ripped in half. She ended up with the head and front legs so technically she won the tug 'o' war, but it wasn't much of a prize. I would have let the crocodile have it at that point. Less to clean up.

Time Travel

If I had a time machine, I'd travel back to 1997 and publish a book about a young wizard named Harry. It wouldn't need to be good, it would just need the characters, plot, and a provable publication date to sue J.K. Rowling in 1998 for plagiarism. I haven't read the book or seen the movie, because I don't give a fuck about magic, but I know Harry has friends named Rob and Herman and they fight a snake.

Tom's Rusty Hinge Story

Holly's father Tom is a story reteller. It doesn't matter how many times he's told a story, or how long it's been since he repeated the story, he will repeat it. I've heard his rusty hinge story eighty-three times.

"Did I tell you I fixed our back door?"
"Yes."
"The hinges were rusty so I bought a tub of Navel Jelly for $6.75 - that's cheaper than buying new hinges for $10."
"Yes, $3.15 cheaper. You could buy a hotdog."
"Excellent stuff that Navel Jelly, took the rust right off. Do you have any rusty hinges?"
"Not at the moment."
"Well, if any get rusty, don't buy new hinges because I still have half a tub of Navel Jelly left. It goes a long way."
"I'll keep that in mind. Thanks."
"No problem. You only need a little bit. No need to slather it on. Takes about ten minutes. It's not just for hinges either, it also works on bolts."
"Really? Bolts don't require a different type of rust remover? One specifically for bolts?"
"No, it also works on bolts. Do you have any rusty bolts?"
"Not that I'm aware of."
"Well, if any get rusty, don't buy new bolts because I still have half of a tub of Navel Jelly left. It goes a long way."

Pottery Barn

I'm not a fan of Pottery Barn. I've only been to one and an old lady asked me to leave because I had my shoes on the bed. Who asks someone to leave just for that? Give them a warning. Also, maybe have a sign stating, *'Bed testers must lie on a weird angle with their shoes hanging off the bed even though that's not how anyone sleeps.'* I suggested such, expecting the old lady to say, "I see your logic and retract my request," but she said, "Don't make me call security."

How Was Your Day?

I read about a study at Harvard in the 1950s, where researchers placed rats in a pool to test how long they could tread water. On average, the rats gave up and sank after 15 minutes. *But...* just before they drowned, the rats were plucked out. Then they were put back in the pool for a second round. This time, the rats treaded water for *sixty* hours. The conclusion drawn was that since the rats believed they would eventually be rescued, they were able to push their bodies way past what they previously thought impossible. I experience the same thing when Holly tells me about her day.

Children

Children just aren't that interesting. There's only so much excitement you can feign over their popsicle stick constructions and ability to wipe their own bum.

"Look, I tied my own shoelaces."
"Good job, I'll contact Mensa immediately and have them send you a membership application."

If they were born with a skill or two, conversations and activities would be less dreadful. Instead of watching cartoons about talking pigs or playing Connect 4, you could build a bookcase or re-tile a bathroom together. My offspring, Seb, spent much of his childhood in a design agency. While other kids were at the park or beach, he attended meetings about typeface options for toaster packaging. He had his own business card and title by the age of five; *Director of Cable Management*. We'd loop a cable around one of his ankles and have him wiggle through crawlspaces far too small for an adult. Once he got stuck and had to be dragged back, another time he was bitten by a rat. Those were his formative years and to this day he can't handle being in tight spaces. He's also not a fan of rats.

Choices

A pack of cigarettes costs around forty dollars in Australia. It's meant to make it difficult for teenagers to take up smoking, but it's also resulted in low-income established smokers choosing nicotine over food for their kids. Which is completely understandable.

"I'm hungry, what's for dinner?"
"Second-hand smoke."
"We had that last night."
"Blame the government. And drink your Coke."
"That's not Coke. It's just a glass of tap water with the word Coke written on the side with a Sharpie."

Tripadvisor

I left a review for a restaurant on Tripadvisor recently. It was the best margherita pizza I've ever had, so I wrote, "Best margherita pizza I've ever had." It was a pretty big statement because I've had some really good ones. After further consideration, I realised someone reading the review might think I haven't had many or was exaggerating, so I added "I've had lots and I'm not exaggerating."

Chevrons

Mike, our creative director, and his partner Patrick had an argument regarding tiles this morning. Apparently Patrick referred to chevron and herringbone tiles as 'identical zigzags', and prefers penny tiles even though it isn't 2004.

"He's design blind. Chevron has 45° angles and Herringbone has 90° angles. That's a big difference."
"Yes, a 45° one."
"Exactly. It's like living with a Neanderthal. Do you know what Patrick calls Frank Lloyd Wright?"
"What?"
"Frank Wright. He says it's pretentious to use the middle name."
"No."
"Yes. And don't get me started on movies. Do you know what his favorite movie is? *Kindergarten Cop*."
"No."
"Yes. He's seen it at least fifty times and he does the, "It's not a tumor!" bit whenever anyone says tumor."
"The word tumor can't possibly come up in conversation that often."
"You'd be surprised. He also does it whenever anyone says 'two more'."

Tall Grass

My best friend at school, Michael, had around fifty washing machines in his backyard. His father repaired them for a living and kept the broken appliances for parts, but most were rusty and hidden by tall grass. Many were stacked two or three high and, if you squinted your eyes, it looked like a city skyline. There was an old couch towards the back of the yard and we ran a couple of sheets of corrugated roofing tin across two stacks of washing machines to make a shelter. It was a good place to hang out until Michael was bitten by a snake and died.

Itinerary

My partner Holly and I have a set itinerary whenever we fly anywhere; I complain about everything and then we have an argument. Once we land and get to the hotel, I'll declare the hotel is a shithole and that I hate whatever country or city we are in. After that, I get badly sunburnt. By the third or fourth day I'm fine and we go out shopping for a fridge magnet. Then we leave the next day on a 4AM flight.

Hike

I read somewhere that the word 'hike' comes from the time when the husband would ride on a mule while the wife had to walk alongside. As the roads were unpaved and muddy, the wife would have to 'hike up her skirt'. If she complained, the husband was allowed to hit her with a stick. If I lived in the seventeenth century, I wouldn't hit my wife with a stick or make her walk alongside my mule. I'd give her the stick and make her walk in front, waving it about to make sure there weren't any spider webs. It can't be that difficult to hike up your dress with one hand.

Dentist

I once sent my dentist a photo of myself trying on a shirt in a changing room with the message, "It fits well but I'm not sure about the colour." The message was intended for Holly, but my dentist replied, "I like the color. Go for it!" I had to find a different dentist after that. Not because of the shirt, it turned out he'd been fondling anaesthetised patients and his clinic was shut down. I was pretty happy about it because I owed them money and wasn't a fan of their waiting room setup.

Salty

My coworker Walter recently discovered Melissa, our front desk human, has been picking her nose and wiping it under her desk. He took a photo as evidence and it looks like a cave with stalactites.

"It's like seven years of snot. Do you want to know how I discovered it?"
"Sure, why not?"
"I tried to tape a USB cable to the underside of her desk, but it wouldn't stick so I got under to have a look and I rubbed it, because I didn't know what it was, and some flakes fell in my mouth. They were salty."

Cargo Shorts

I'm a big fan of cargo shorts. I wore them to a wedding once. I'd wear them year-round if I could, but my calves get cold around October. I realize cargo shorts also come in pant length, but I wouldn't be seen dead in cargo pants. I know a guy named Nick who wears cargo pants and he shoots pumpkins behind his trailer with an AR-15 semi-automatic rifle.

Math

I don't do math. I've never been able to. I'm probably slightly retarded or something, but I don't work in an industry where I need to triangulate circle trajectories or calculate the square root of houses, so I don't care. I remember being told as a child, "You won't always have a calculator on you," but that statement seems a bit shortsighted now.

"Hello? Mrs Lawson?
"Yes, who is this?"
"It's David Thorne. I was in your math class in 1982."
"I'm sorry, I've taught a lot of kids over the years."
"I'm sure you have. Did you tell all of them they wouldn't always have a calculator on them?"
"Sorry?"
"Wait, let me just check my phone... 7 x 8 is 56, Mrs Lawson. You must feel pretty fucking stupid now."

Poutine

Canadian's really need to stop bragging about poutine. It's gravy and cheese curds on fries and the kind of thing you could make by mistake.

Wills

I've never been bequeathed anything in a will. I've seen television shows where family members sit in a lawyer's office listening in anticipation as a will is read, but they're generally families with money. Someone gets bequeathed a mansion and someone else vows they'll fight it in court. A will reading for anyone in my family would sound like someone who works at Goodwill listing off the contents of a box left at the back door.

"And to David, I bequeath my four-slice toaster, eight teaspoons, and a fitted sheet."

Hall & Oats

Whenever my partner Holly and I disagree about something and I know I'm wrong, I change the facts on Wikipedia to side with my error and then tell her to look it up.

"Well I'll be, Tom Sellek of *Magnum P.I.* fame *was* in the band Hall & Oats. I apologise for doubting you. I just figured the band name was made up of their last names."

Wigs

My father had a lot of affairs. At least five that I know of. My mother made him sleep in a tent in the backyard whenever it happened - the amount of nights depended on how long it took my father to convince my mother she was to blame for letting herself go and how attractive the woman he slept with was.

"Yes, we could go to marriage counselling again, that's one option, *or* we could spend the money on wigs."
"Wigs?"
"Yes, a bunch of wigs for you to wear."
"What kind of wigs?"
"All the kinds. Coloured ones, curly ones, maybe a long blonde crimply one like Darryl Hannah in *Splash*."
"Darryl Hannah?"
"I'm just using her as an example. Lots of people have long blonde crimply hair. Your sister for example."

Crows

A lot has been documented about the intelligence of crows. I read about a test once where they placed a crow in a room with a dismantled engine block from a 2006 Toyota Camry, and it built a robot exoskeleton and escaped by blasting through a concrete wall.

Sinkhole

The suburb I grew up in had a sinkhole. Technically it wasn't a real sinkhole, just a deep bog, but it was fenced with warning signs because a kid had drowned there. I climbed over the fence once but I didn't stay long because there was ghost story going around about the kid who drowned coming out of the water and dragging you in. There were also a lot of mosquitos.

PTSD

I visited Petco last week, to buy dog food, and decided to look in the lizard and turtle section. As I peered into a glass enclosure to see whether it contained a lizard or turtle, a tarantula the size of my hand jumped at the glass. Why would anyone put a tarantula in the lizard and turtle section? It should have its own section. I knocked over a stand of aquarium decorations as I went backwards and broke four Squidward houses. I'll have to avoid the lizard and turtle section now, which is annoying because I like lizards and turtles. And, before you state, "That's not PTSD!", while I was looking out our kitchen window this morning, a bird flew into the glass, and a mug I was holding dented the ceiling.

Pharmaceuticals

There are a lot of advertisements for pharmaceutical drugs on American television. Watching an episode of *Jeopardy* will subject you to at least twenty different commercials featuring old people finally able to push their grandkids on a swing thanks to drugs with names like Ethdytrin or Apibatipopyol. There's so many drug brands that the marketing teams have given up bothering to come up with clever names and adopted the Scrabble bag shake, dump, and run with it approach.

"What's this drug do?"
"It reduces sun glare by 2%."
"Any side effects?"
"Depression, loss of vision, paralysis and death, but we'll mention that soothingly in the commercial."
"What are we going to call it?"
"Fsdfwjffdghrte. Keith came up with it when he had a stroke while typing. He's on medication that thins nose hairs."

Adhesive Nipples

My friend Andrew has no left nipple. Apparently it's a medical condition called Athelia and there's a large market for rubber adhesive nipples. He has packs of five at home and keeps a couple in the glove box of his car. They're not cheap either, I stuck one to my cheek once and he made me give him thirty-five dollars.

Plumbing

I once left my sunglasses at my friend Geoffrey's house and went back to get them. I'd only been gone a few minutes, so I didn't bother to knock, and walked in to witness Geoffrey pooing in a trashcan. It was one of those flip-up lid trashcans and Geoffrey was squatting over it, naked from the waist down, pressing the foot pedal with his hand. As he leapt up in surprise, the lid closed and a half-out log broke off and landed on top. Nothing prepares you for this, so I kind of froze and just stood there staring at the poo on the lid while Geoffrey yelled at me. Apparently the plumbing in his toilet wasn't working, but who poos in a trashcan? Poo in the shower and waffle-stomp those nuggets down the drain like the rest of us.

ISIS

I'm not a huge fan of ISIS. You'd think they'd have better things to do than driving around in the back of Toyota pickups waving guns and yelling, "Wololololol!" Like cleaning. I've seen where they live and there's a lot of rubble. I get that it's good to have a hobby and clubs provide camaraderie, but ISIS take themselves way too seriously. It's probably difficult to keep a sense of humour when you live in a cave though.

"Good morning, Afukghar."
"Morning, Jahgrahar, how did you sleep?"
"Not well, I was stung by scorpions several times."
"Yes, there are many scorpions in our cave."
"I have a joke for you."
"You do? Please tell it."
"Okay, I've started a business crafting tiny figurines of Muhammad."
"You have?"
"Yes, it's making small prophets."
"That isn't funny and because you blasphemed, you must now be beheaded."
"I knew the repercussions. I can't spend another night in the scorpion cave."

Dining Tables

I'm not sure why we have a dining table in our house. It only gets used once a year for Christmas dinner, and everyone hates it. I've seen festive scenes on television where people laugh gaily as they pass the mashed potato, but there's not a lot of that happening at our Christmas dinners. It's mostly just statements about how long it's been since we last used the dining table. If good meals are based on good company and good conversation, the best we can hope for is a quick meal. The dining table was also used for a jigsaw puzzle once, but nobody here wants to go through that again. It had a lot of trees. I think it was a Bavarian castle.

Hulu

I hate scrolling through fifteen different streaming services, all with different interfaces, attempting to find something vaguely watchable. Most of the streaming services don't even use the proper cover image, they make their own, so you'll be scrolling and think, "Ooh, what's this?" but then it turns out to be *Friends* or a documentary about Alexandre-Ferdinand Godefroy, the inventor of the hair dryer.

Aquaman's Mom

Why is Nicole Kidman in anything? She's nobody's favourite actress and no director has ever stated, "You know who'd be perfect for this role? Nicole Kidman." Perhaps she just turns up on set uninvited like she does at red carpet events.

"And there's Meryl Street looking absolutely gorgeous in a blue Karl Lagerfeld gown, perhaps we can g..."
"G'day!"
"Oh, it's Nicole Kidman. What a surprise."
"Yes, I'm bonza excited to be here. Keith couldn't join me this evening, because he's working on a song about dusty paddocks, but he's watching at home in Australia from his shoebox."
"Okay, so if you could just head off that wa..."
"I'm wearing Armani."
"Look, I don't mean to be rude, Nicole, but I'm really going to need you to..."
"Yes, I'm extremely excited about my latest movie role. I play Aquaman's mom."
"Wait. You're in the movie *Aquaman*? I didn't know that. You weren't in the trailer."
"It's my biggest role since penguin #28 in *Happy Feet*."

Facebook

I'm not a big fan of Facebook as it's mostly people posting photos of things they did without me. A photo of a cat? Didn't need to be there and the cat looks like every other cat. A photo of people I know drinking beer around a camp fire? I hope someone throws a bag of gunpowder and nails in.

Excuses

I've had to come up with a lot of excuses for missed deadlines over the last thirty years. I've had about forty dogs put down, an auntie die in a tractor accident, a nephew get washed off rocks, and my offspring, Seb, losing his sight after being spat at by a snake. I don't even care if the excuses are believable at this point, what are they going to do about it?

"Your wife Holly is having emergency surgery for brain swelling after being hit on the head by a coconut?"
"Yes, it's far more common than you'd think."
"It is?"
"It's more common than moose attacks."
"I wasn't aware Virginia even has coconut trees."
"It was a washed up coconut. Someone threw it."

Log Cabins

Sometimes I imagine simply walking away from all my responsibilities. I'd leave my phone and wallet behind and head to a forest - maybe do a few farm chores in exchange for food on the way - and build myself a log cabin. I'd probably need a few supplies, like an axe and a book on building log cabins, so I would actually take my wallet. That would also save me having to do farm chores; I doubt it's all ponytailed farm ladies who lost their husband in a tractor accident saying, "Well, there's a fence that needs fixing, are you any good with a hammer?", there's probably also quite a bit of lifting involved. And poo.

"Hello farm lady, I was wandering past and thought I'd stop to ask if you have any chores you need doing in exchange for a meal?"
"Well, the cow shed could do with a really good poo-scraping."
"I'm more of a fence-fixing wanderer actually, you don't have any fences in disrepair?"
"No, just lots of poo."
"I'll be on my way then. Sorry to bother you."

Signs

When I was nine, I recorded myself saying "Hello, my name is David and this is how I sound when I talk through a comb with a piece of tissue paper wrapped around it," over my father's cassingle of *Stayin' Alive*. It was discovered during the next family drive and my punishment was to stand at the entrance of our driveway holding a sign that read, "I have no respect for other people's property." Holding a sign was a common punishment in our household. I'd informed the neighbourhood of several offences over the years, including: "I stole $10 from my mother's purse to buy a plastic sword", "I swapped my sister's bike for a Penthouse magazine", and, "Honk if you dislike liars; I told my teacher my parents died."

The Classics

I've never been a fan of 'the classics'. I once had to read Alcott's *Little Women* for a school assignment and I figure that's enough of the Classics to keep me going for a while. It mostly consisted of girls talking about their feelings and complaining about things. There was also a guy who rode a horse.

Magic Mushrooms

I tried magic mushrooms when I was nineteen. I don't think they were the right kind. My friend Thomas and I drove into the Adelaide hills, jumped a wire fence, and picked the first mushrooms we found - they had red spots like a Smurf house and tasted like metal. I only had a small nibble but ended up on life-support for three days due to my nervous system shutting down. Thomas ate four mushrooms; he actually died in the ambulance on the way to hospital but was brought back. He wasn't the same afterwards though; his movements were twitchy and he wore pyjama pants out of the house. I asked him if he'd seen anything while he was dead, like a bright tunnel with Jesus at the end, and he said the only thing he remembered was riding a giant moth to a supermarket. I was also twitchy, but only for about three months, and not as twitchy as Thomas - I could drink a glass of water without spilling it, and walk without looking like a horse counting. Mostly it was just like living in a slow frame rate. Also, I was a bit healthier than Thomas to begin with, he huffed a lot of whipped cream cylinders. I tried it once but it was just thirty seconds of *womp* sounds and I wet myself.

How Is That a Tango?

Kate, our HR manager, was a contestant on the local version of *Dancing With the Stars* last week. She's not a star, by any stretch of the imagination, but that didn't matter because nobody was. The biggest star was a lady who owns a bakery. Kate and her dancing partner, an old guy named Dick, did an awkward tango comprising entirely of Dick clicking his fingers above his head while Kate walked around him for three minutes. I voted for someone else, I couldn't vote for that. At the end of Kate's dance, when the host asked a few contrived questions, Kate declared, "This has been a dream come true." Pretty shitty dream. I had a dream about a talking mouse last week that was heaps better.

Spare Room

Staying with friends or relatives when you travel never works out cheaper because you have to take them out to dinner and the bill will be $457.80. Also, you'll have to share a room with a treadmill and two filing cabinets, and you'll run out of things to talk about by 7pm but they'll make you sit around their fire pit listening to Bruce Springsteen until 10pm.

Wrong Number

I once collected my offspring and two of his classmates from after-school lacrosse practice. The boys were siblings and their mother, Terri, knew I'd be dropping them home afterwards. Regardless, I sent her a message to let her know the boys were with me, but accidently sent a guy named Terry, a work client, the message, "I have your kids."

Love Gun

My sister had a boyfriend in the eighties, named Trevor, who owned a van with the members of KISS painted on the side. He liked giving me dead arms and that thing where you rub a knuckle on the top of someone's head, so I pooed in a bag and wiped it into the air vents of his van. He died in a crash a few days later. Not because of the poo; he was low on fuel, so switched the vehicle off to coast down a big hill, and when he tried to turn at the bottom, the steering lock engaged. He went through the front window of a H&R Block and was decapitated by a giant green square. I caught a bus with my sister to his funeral. They played *Love Gun*.

The CEO of Levers

Our front desk human, Melissa, once told a client on the telephone that Mike, our creative director, wasn't available because he was at the hairdresser. It was apparently the worst thing that had ever happened to Mike and several stern emails were written. Now, whenever a client calls for Mike and he's not in the office, Melissa has to say, "I'm sorry, Mike is in a meeting with the CEO of Unilever." It's written on a post-it note stuck to the reception desk because she once forgot the Uni part of Unilever and said, "I'm sorry, Mike is in a meeting with the CEO of levers."

"How fucking hard is it to remember Unilever? It's one of the largest brands on the planet."
"Not everyone cares about pens."
"What?"
"Unilever make pens."
"No they don't."
"I'm using one."
"That's a fucking Uniball."
"Oh, I might have been saying Uniball then because I don't look at the post-it note, I look at my pen."
"Are you serious?"
"Maybe you just shouldn't tell lies."

Old Blossom

I'm not a fan of old Blossom. Who dresses her? Is she cosplaying Angela Lansbury? Why is she hosting Jeopardy? Nobody wants to hear her quips after every answer; we know she has the answers written down for her and it's almost as annoying as her hair.

"The daguerreotype?"
"Correct. Invented by Louise Daguerre in 1839. Also, I don't just play a scientist on television, I have a philosophy degree in neuroscience."
"Do you have any peer-reviewed publications?"
"Yes, *Mayim's Vegan Table*, containing 100 vegan recipes, is available on Amazon. And that takes us to a break."

I shouldn't belittle anyone's academic achievements. I'm sure old Blossom is a great neuroscientist. She probably spends her weekends in her shed working on a cure for Alzheimer's or Parkinson's disease when she's not out shopping in thrift stores for lightly-worn shoes.

"Hello, Michael J. Fox? This is old Blossom, I've discovered a cure for Parkinsons. The active ingredient is cat hair."

Walter's Bike

My coworker Walter denounces motor vehicles as a socially irresponsible form of transport. Unless he has to go somewhere that is too far to ride. Other people's motor vehicles are fine then. He won't offer to pay for petrol though because that supports companies who make dolphins sew sneakers for less than minimum wage. If I'm on my way to work and see Walter riding, I drive past really close and sound my horn. Usually it just makes him wobble a bit but he fell off once.

Pointy Sticks

Sometimes during production meetings, I like to imagine what it would be like if we were all marooned on a tropical island and had to survive. There'd probably be a lengthy discussion about a rock shaped like a frog on the first day, with fire and shelter mentioned as future actionable items. We'd go to sleep cold and hungry, but confident we had a strategy to move forward with. On the third day we'd eat Melissa, and that night I'd stab everyone with a pointy stick while they were sleeping just in case I was next.

Night Wasps

My family owned a caravan when I was young. It wasn't a nice caravan, it was more rust than metal and you had to poo in a bucket while holding a towel up in front of yourself. My cousin Susan came on vacation with us once, and when she realised it was mostly just playing Uno and pooing in a bucket three-feet away from everyone else, she cried and begged to go home. My father made her a bed in the back of our station wagon and, for three days, Susan only came out to eat, frown, and use the bucket. I was quite annoyed by this because I'd asked several times if I could sleep in the station wagon and was told, "No, there isn't enough air in there for a whole night and you can't have a window down because night wasps will get in and lay eggs in your ears."

Interestingly, Susan developed an ear infection shortly after the vacation. It was so bad that she ended up in the hospital and permanently lost hearing in one ear. I was fully convinced it was due to night wasp eggs and, up until I was about twelve, slept with rolled up bits of tissue paper in my ears.

Professor Television

My offspring Seb got a job at Best Buy last month and now he's an expert on refresh rates. I call him Professor Television because every conversation is about specs only people into plugs and dakimakura care about.

"And that's just thirty reasons why you should buy the Sony Spazmatron. Additionally, it has 1200 quadbikes of nanotoasters and a refresh rate of 9000 gigaberries. That's important for watching shows about tin."
"Seb, it's 3am. I was having a nice dream about horses."

Tin Tin

My teacher in fourth-grade, Mrs Easton, once told the class that camels store water in their humps. Camel humps contain fat reserves, not water. I knew this from reading *The Crab with the Golden Claws,* a Tin Tin book. When I informed her she was wrong, Mrs Easton made me stand outside. I leaned far more from reading Tin Tin than I ever learned in Mrs Easton's class. Tin Tin taught me that sometimes all you need is a great coat and a good companion, Mrs Easton taught me that not all fat women are jolly.

County Fairs

Holly tricked me into going to a county fair last week. Lynyrd Skynyrd was playing and she told me he was a rave DJ. It wasn't a he, it was a group of old guys in denim jackets singing about birds. I was the only guy there that didn't have a belt knife.

Magnification

Holly bought a X10 magnifying mirror last week, and I've decided I'm never standing within twenty feet of anyone ever again. Apparently I've had a thick black hair growing out of one of my manhole-sized nose pores for six months. It looks like a piece of licorice.

"There's a thick black hair growing out of my nose."
"Yes, it's hard to miss."
"What? How long has it been there?"
"I don't know, six months."
"And you didn't think to mention it?"
"I figured you'd seen it."
"And what, I decided to keep it? To see how long it would get? Why would I do that?"
"Who knows why you do half the things you do."

Immortality

Aging happens and probably will until we learn to harvest jellyfish DNA and turn it into a pill. We'll need to cure arthritis before that though. And Alzheimers. What's the point of living forever if you can't open a jar without a special tool or remember why you're standing in a warehouse holding a sword?

Golf

I'm not a fan of golf. I find it boring. Maybe it's more about *who* you play golf with than playing though. I've only ever played once and that was with my friend JM and his geriatric golfing buddies. One of them, a guy named Chuck, collects civil war uniform buttons.

"And do you know what this is?"
"Another button?"
"It's the button off a confederate officer's dress uniform, circa 1862. You can identify the year by the ridges. Buttons manufactured after March 1863 were stamped without the ridges. Buttons manufactured before 1862 also had ridges, but the spacing between the ridges is slightly wider. And do you know what this is?"
"Another button?"

Product Research

Whenever my coworker Ben states, "I'll have the copy to you by tomorrow," it means he will start working on it next week, possibly the week after, if everyone leaves him alone. Copywriters don't care about deadlines... No, actually, they don't care about *other people's* deadlines. They like having copy deadlines because it gives them a set amount of time not to do it until the last moment. I walked into Ben's office this afternoon, to see how he was going with copy I've been waiting two weeks for, and he was watching the movie *Wonder Woman 1984* with the lights off.

"How is this product research?"
"The packaging I'm writing the copy for has an eighties color palette. I'm watching this for the pop-culture references."
"Really, Ben?"
"Yes. Also, watch this... hang on, I'll rewind it a bit... there, did you see that?"
"See what?"
"When Wonder Woman jumped over the truck. Her dress lifted up and you could see her underwear."

Butter

My coworker Gary was late this morning because his cat ate a stick of butter. Apparently he had to wait for the cat to poo. Walter, our junior designer, asked, "Did it poo out the whole stick of butter?" and Gary replied, "No, don't be stupid." Walter then explained that he didn't mean an intact stick of butter, because cats are warm, and Gary told him to leave his office.

Mr Mercury

I had a teacher named Mr Mercury in fourth grade. He was a fan of the band Queen and loved it when people asked if he was related to Freddie. He said he was, and that Freddie had been to his house, but I've learned since that Freddie Mercury's real name was Farrokh Bulsara, so I call bullshit. Mr Mercury also told us that he could hold his breath underwater for five minutes, but who can trust anything he said? I saw him at a basketball game several years later and I thought about saying something, but he was a couple of seats down and he'd lost a hand somehow. He had one of those attachments with a stainless steel claw and pulleys.

Patterns

My partner Holly puts paper towel rolls on the holder upside down. We've spoken about it at least a hundred times, so I'm fairly certain she only does it to annoy me. Right-handed people tear off a paper towel to the left; it keeps the action tight and across the body - you don't tear to the right, that's just flailing your arm out into no-man's land. A glass of wine could be knocked over or you could strain a surprised muscle. Nobody wants to do a backhand tennis swing just to get a paper towel. Also, sometimes she buys the ones with printed patterns. I can't do paper towel patterns; it changes the whole look of the kitchen. Once she bought paper towels with starfish on them even though we don't live anywhere near a beach.

"Ahoy, can you pass me a paper towel featuring starfish please?"
"They were out of plain ones. I told you that."
"It's fine, I like them. We should redo the entire kitchen in a marine theme. Maybe add a porthole."
"You do carry on a bit."
"Beach hair, don't care. Can you also pass me the potato peeler?"
'Where is it?'
"Starboard drawer."

Carl

My neighbour Carl spends all day sitting on his deck, defending his vegetable garden from squirrels with an .22 rifle. Each time he murders one, he raises a fist in the air and yells, "Wayhey!" He then strips, smears the blood of his hunt over his naked body, and masturbates. Okay, that last bit isn't true but as I doubt Carl will ever read this, I can write what I want. Once, I saw him sucking off a small boy behind his garden shed.

Slazenger

Our house burned down when I was ten; it was a bar heater and dressing gown thing. We had nothing but the clothes we were wearing and my father's Slazenger.

"Is that what you ran back in for? Your tennis racquet?"
"It's signed by John McEnroe."
"No, it isn't. That's just a sticker. Why didn't you save our wedding album and family photos?"
"Let's not worry about that, they're just possessions. The important thing is that everyone is okay."
"Everyone and your tennis racquet."
"I have a semi finals match next week."

Mini-Stroke

I had a chatty cashier at Lowes this morning and I wasn't ready for it. I need prep time for conversations. "It's getting warm outside," she said, "It will be summer before we know it." For some reason, I decided the word *indubitably* was an appropriate response, but as I said it my brain had a mini-stroke and it came out as "Indo bibly bibly." The cashier stared at me strangely and I decided my only recourse was to pretend I speak another language, so I added, "Bibly albib oobibly." Remembering a few words from French lessons at school, I also threw in "la pomme" which I think means 'the apple'.

"Will that be all for you today sir?"
"Bibly."
"Your total is $12.98, do you have a Lowe's card?"
"Bib."
"Credit or debit?"
"Bebit."
"Would you like the receipt in the bag?"
"Bibly."
"Have a nice day."
"Bib boo."

Emergency

I read somewhere that if you are ever in a violent situation, you should dial the police and order a large pizza. It doesn't work the other way; you can't call Pizza Hut and ask for the police, and you have to be home. It won't work if you're hiking and meet a bear.

800% Pleased

Often when we take on new clients, Mike, our creative director, gives them a tour of the agency. He likes us to act busy and pretend we're professional. Once, he told our account manager Gary to pretend he was on a call and say, "We don't have the final numbers, but early results show an 800% increase in sales... yes, I'll let Mike and the team know how pleased you are." Gary messed up his lines and said, "Mike will be 800% pleased about those numbers," and for the next few months, whenever Mike stated he was pleased about anything, I'd ask, "Okay, but are you 800% pleased?" Some things don't require more than one person to find them hilarious. It's like when you see an ambulance rushing somewhere with its siren on and say, "They'll never sell any ice cream going that fast."

Outback Steakhouse

Holly's father Tom won't eat mushrooms because they're too exotic. His idea of fancy international cuisine is Outback Steakhouse; it's posh because they bring you a wooden board with a loaf of black bread on it. He won't eat the bread, because bread is meant to be white and sliced, but he likes the battered and fried' sliced onions. I refuse to call them Bloomin' Onions, because it's stupid. All of their dish names are stupid. I'm not asking for Sydney Shrooms or Kookaburra Wings. It's like opening an American themed restaurant in Australia with dishes called the Mobility Scooter Burger and Bald Eagle Wings.

"Welcome to the No Healthcare Steakhouse. Would you care to try the Freedom Dip?"
"What is it?"
It's a neon-yellow block of cheese with candy corns poked into it. A very popular dish in America. They all eat it."
"No, I'll have the Guantánamo Bay Guacamole."

Outback Steakhouse's slogan is 'no rules' so technically you're allowed to take the cutlery. We have about twenty of their steak knives and three wooden bread boards at our house Also a big poster of an old stamp.

Homeless People

If I were homeless, I'd move to Hawaii. If I have to sleep outside, I'd like a nice view and comfortable climate. I'd relax and swim during the day, and wander into beach luaus for a slice of rotisserie pig in the evenings. Larger luaus obviously, ones where an extra guest won't be noticed, not the ones with log seat circles and some dickhead playing a guitar.

Nuhughn

I once worked with a deaf guy named Neil. We were in different departments - he was an account rep and I worked in the art department - but we often had to drive to attend client meetings together. The trips were excruciating as he drove a manual car and never went above second gear. The engine screamed and the rev counter redlined while he sat there oblivious. If I tried to tell him, he'd just smile and say, "Nuhughn." We were running late one day and, after pushing his car harder than usual, a cylinder punched through the hood and flames came out the air-conditioning vents. Also, if you can't hear people knocking on your office door, maybe lock it if you're planning on having a lunch wank.

Patchouli

I lived in a sharehouse when I was at uni and one of my housemates had a girlfriend named Rebecca. She was an art student and wore a lot of patchouli oil. All art students wear patchouli oil as it's a magic repellant against criticism. Rebecca was annoying in the way that all art students are annoying; poor and devoid of actual talent. We had one of her paintings on our living room wall titled *Self Portrait 28*. Nobody wanted the painting in the house, she hung it while we were out.

"So, it's you on a horse?"
"It's an expression of joy, movement, and freedom."
"Shouldn't the horse be in motion then?"
"It *is* in motion."
"Its legs would be bent if it was in motion."
"It's jumping."
"Straight up?"
"It's easy to criticise."
"Correct."
"An inability to interpret art says a lot more about the viewer than the artist. It's not my job to explain."
"Granted. You weren't overly helpful with the title though, you should have called it *Rebecca's Happy Hover Horse*."

Singing Bowls

We have 26 brass singing bowls in our house. Holly kept ordering them from Amazon until she found one she liked the tone of. I use one for cereal, others are distributed about the house to collect things in. Dead moths mainly.

Pho

I tried pho for the first time tonight and I'm not a fan. I'd rather eat a Maggi packet noodle soup. At least the packet soup has some flavour. I'm not sure who came up with pho but they should have kept it to themselves.

"So I take rice noodles and chopped veggies..."
"And cook them?"
"Kind of, I drop them in tepid bone broth before serving."
"Right..."
"That's it."
"There's no flavouring?"
"It's tepid bone broth flavour."
"Okay, so it's basically the saddest soup imaginable. Is there at least bread to dip in it?"
"No."

Country Music

My friend JM is a big country music fan. His favourite song is about a guy who drives his pickup to collect his mother from prison, but before he gets there, she's run over by a train. It's pretty much up there with the classics like *Achy Breaky Heart* by Hannah Montana's dad and Kenny Chesney's *She Thinks My Tractor's Sexy*. For those not familiar with *She Thinks My Tractor's Sexy*, here are the lyrics:

Plowing these fields in the hot summer sun.
Over by the gate yonder here she comes.
With a basket full of chicken and a big cold jug of sweet tea.
I make a little room and she climbs on up,
I open up the throttle and stir a little dust.
Look at her face, she ain't a foolin' me,
she thinks my tractor's sexy.
It really turns her on.

It's basically the music equivalent of *Fifty Shades of Grey* for farmers. Yes, Cletus, everyone thinks your tractor is hot. When you're blocking traffic doing 15mph on a single lane road, we're definitely all thinking, "I'd love to give that tractor driver some chicken," and not, "Pull over and let me pass you leather-faced old cunt."

Once a Designer

It's said that it's never too late to change careers, but graphic designers always become old graphic designers. Some attempt to escape, but other graphic designers are sent after them with a nice grid or clever logo to bring them back into the fold.

"I hate design, I hate other designers, and I hate everything about the industry. I finally managed to escape and I'm happy for the first time in my life."
"Good for you. What do you think of this logotype?"
"Hmm. Kerning could do with some work. The spacing between the D and O in particular are... dammit!"
"Get in the van."

Venmo

Our senior designer, Jodie, has been taking Ozempic for several months, but hasn't lost any weight because it turned out to be a cheap Chinese knockoff. It was some kind of bean juice. She ordered it online and had to use Venmo, so you'd think that would've been a red flag. There's always something sketchy going on if you have to pay with Venmo. It's mainly just for poppers, sandwich bag weed, and Denny's parking lot handjobs.

Poland

Political correctness wasn't a thing in Australian schools during the eighties. Teachers smacked you on the back of the head as they walked down aisles, smoked in class, and called you a poofter if you were bad at sports. Just a few years earlier, teachers were allowed to cane students, so perhaps robbed of the right to physically scar children, they were lashing out in the only way they had left. My history teacher once told me that my parents should have aborted me because I couldn't find Poland on a map. Who the fuck knows where Poland is on a map?

"And which historic war or battle did you choose to write about for your class presentation, David?"
"The Battle of Hoth."
"Hmm. I don't recall that one. Please continue."
"A long time ago, in a galaxy far, far away..."
"Outside. I don't want to see your face again today."
"It's raining."
"Good, please catch pneumonia and die. Okay, next up is Allison. Have you done the assignment, Allison?"
"No."
"Of course you haven't, you toothless halfwit. I met your parents at last week's parent-teacher night and it was patently obvious they're siblings."

Large Properties

It's annoying that all of the 'fun' Americans I know are rednecks. They're the ones that ride ATVs, shoot guns, and drink bourbon. None of the liberal Americans I know have fun, they're far too busy being offended by everything, and none of them own large properties.

"What have you been up to, Ben?"
"Well, I recently started a petition against large belt buckles. Anything above two inches is simply a display of toxic masculinity. I also started my own blog called *Whispered Screams*, a collection of my poetry. Would you like to hear my latest? It's titled *Someone Stole My Black Lives Matter Sign*."
"No thanks."

Apple II

When I was nine, an old guy on a bus invited me to his house to see his Apple II. He did have an Apple II and we played *Lode Runner*, but we also traced our penises onto a piece of paper with a pen. Apparently I did it wrong so he had to trace mine for me. The trick is to pull the foreskin back so you have a more defined edge to trace, or it will just look like a silo with a bump.

Money Sock

I'm fully aware of my faults and the only logical reason I can think of for why Holly hasn't left me yet, is she assumes I have money hidden somewhere and is waiting for the moment I say, "Well done, you passed the test, I'm not really this dreadful, I just needed to know if you love me for who I am or are just in it for the money." Like that Elvis movie where he swaps his sports car for a motorbike and teaches watersports.

"Please, you don't have any money."
"Yes I do, Holly, it was all just a cunning ploy."
"You pretended to be broke for fourteen years?"
"A cunning and lengthy ploy."
"Where's this money hidden then?"
"In my sock drawer. Inside a sock I sometimes wear to give the impression that it's no different from any of my other socks. I put the money in a different sock when I wear the money sock."
"Are you talking about the fuzzy blue sock with four-hundred dollars in it?"
"Four-hundred and twenty-five dollars actually."

Parking Pass

When I was at uni, a guy named Matthew Buchanan stole a colour scanner from the computer room. I saw him put it in his Ford Fiesta. A hundred dollar reward was offered for information about the theft, so I made Matthew give me a hundred dollars and his parking pass not to tell. It's not like we were friends, I saw him throw rocks at a goose once.

RV Adventure

We lost an employee this year. Not in the sense of them quitting or dying, but we don't know where Rebecca our production manager is. A few months back, she stated she was going to "work remotely for a bit" and just never came back. She had some stuff going on, but that's no reason not to clearly state, "I discovered my husband prefers the company of men, so I emptied our bank account, bought an RV, and am driving across America. It won't affect my work." The first we learned of Rebecca's RV adventure is when she joined a Zoom call from the Niagara Falls visitor center parking lot. Every Zoom call since has been from a parking lot. Most of them have been Walmart parking lots though.

Ayers Rock

I visited Alice Springs with my friend Bill in 2005 and we climbed a big rock. Not all the way to the top, as it was quite steep, but we got the idea. You're not allowed to climb the big rock anymore, because it makes ghosts sad, so there's zero point visiting Alice Springs now. There is a resort with a pool shaped like a crocodile, but it doesn't look like a crocodile when you're there, just from the air. Maybe I'm just hard to impress; Bill liked Alice Springs more than I did. Partly because a pool assistant named Cody let Bill suck him off inside a floatie shed. I had no idea at the time but I did wonder why it took them so long to pick out the big frosted donut.

"You couldn't decide, Bill?"
"About what?"
"The floatie. The shed's not that big. What were there, like ten floaties to choose from? Also, the $200 tip was a bit extravagant."
"It was worth every cent."
"You were only on it for five minutes."
"Best five minutes of the trip."
"Really? I might have a go then... no, too late, that kid is on it now."

Verizon

After fifteen years of stating, "I need a keypad," Holly's parents, Maria and Tom, caved and got their first smart phones last week. Maria even delved into her settings and now has a photo of Donald Trump playing golf as her background. She tried to show Tom how to do it but somehow reset his phone to factory settings and he had to go back to AT&T. A teenage girl behind the counter told him there was a two-hour wait and he yelled at her and was asked to leave. He says he's going to switch over to Verizon.

Party Invites

I once told a kid at school that I was having a birthday party even though it was nowhere near my birthday. I have no idea why. Word got around and cornered by the lie, I invited about forty kids. I was enjoying the attention at that point. I even gave out invites with my address and a date set several weeks away, figuring this would give me time to come up with an excuse for cancelling. I forgot all about it until the first guests arrived. My father was watching cricket on television while my mother was out doing the weekly shopping.

The Phantom

I was a big fan of *The Phantom* comics when I was a kid. I even made myself a Phantom costume. It was just my sister's jazzercise leotard and a mask constructed by cutting eye holes in a sweater sleeve, but I felt it was pretty convincing. I imagined stopping a crime and, while being interviewed on the news, taking off my mask and saying "It's me!" to the shock and awe of all the kids at my school. That night, after my parents had gone to bed, I put on the costume and climbed out my window. It was darker and scarier than I expected, our village didn't have street lights. Deciding to enlist my friend Ashley as my sidekick, I jumped his back fence and tapped on his bedroom window. Ashley opened his curtains, peered out, and I put a finger to my lips and said, "Shhhh." I probably should have taken the mask off first. Ashley's drawing of the person he saw outside his window was printed in the local newspaper a few days later. It was pretty bad, like a corncob with eyes. A police officer also visited our class to warn us about securing our doors and windows at night and asked if anyone recognised the person in Ashley's drawing. Rather unimpressed with the likeness, I put my hand up and stated, "If Ashley wasn't such a bad drawer, it would probably look a lot like The Phantom."

Board Games

I don't like board games. They take ages to set up and put away and the bit between requires a lot of leaning over. Out of all the board games I've played, Trivial Pursuit is, by far, the worst. It takes fifteen days to play. The last time I played Trivial Pursuit, with Holly's parents and her brother, I thought I was going to die. My eyes rolled back in my head and I felt my body just giving up as I waited the four hours for my turn. When Holly's brother finally won, I actually sobbed with relief. As I began to pack up, Holly's father stopped me and said, "No, we play on to see who comes second."

Sleep Number

Holly took me mattress shopping recently but there's no way I can properly test a mattress when the salesman is standing a foot away staring down at me. I don't care if it's a coil-foam hybrid, go sit behind your little desk and I'll call you over when I need to know if you have a mattress as comfortable as the 10K Hästens Excelsior for around three hundred. Also, fuck Sleep Number, I'm not paying 6K for a blowup mattress. I can get a Coleman blowup mattress for forty bucks.

Home Haircuts

So you've decided to cut your own hair. Good for you. You're embarking on a journey of discovery and savings the whole family can enjoy. Before you begin this journey, you will need to purchase a set of clippers. Wal-Mart carries a large range of Wahl brand electric clippers, but I prefer the Oster Classic 76 Professional because I'm not poor.

Cutting your children's hair

Go for it. They're never going to let you cut their hair again, so get creative. This is an excellent opportunity to discover what the different length blade-combs do and learn from your mistakes.

Cutting your own hair

Step 1. State you are only going to 'clean it up a bit'.
Step 2. Cut it way too short.
Step 3. Don't leave the house for two weeks.
Step 4. Swear that you are never going to cut it that short again.
Step 5. Repeat.

Boyfriend

If I were gay, I'd select a boyfriend my height to save having to readjust my car's driver's seat position. I'm not interested in doubling my wardrobe as I wear the same outfit everyday to facilitate speedy identification should I ever be in a boating accident.

Patrick Rafter

Early in my career, when I was still doing freelance, I was commissioned to put together a book titled *Learn To Play Tennis With Patrick Rafter*. Patrick had just won the US Open and the publisher wanted the book on shelves within two-weeks. Which may seem like a reasonable deadline, but I had to take the photos, do the layout, *and* write the book. Pages 20 to 37 just contain mathematical formulas for calculating wind speed that I copied from a meteorological website, and the photos of Patrick's hand holding a tennis racket are me holding a broom. When I met Patrick to take the photographs, he was a bit of a dick and told me, "I don't know why I agreed to do this, you've got five minutes." Hence the broom photos and the bit in his bio about collecting pinecones and having a pet sheep named Sheryl.

Proposal

I proposed to my partner Holly while we were playing tennis, and she's never let me forget it. Maybe I should have written, "Holly will you marry me?" in tennis balls, but I only had five. Sorry I'm not a coach. When other women describe the romantic situation in which they were proposed to and ask Holly how I did it, she gives me a pursed lip glance and lies.

"And as Jeff and I watched the sun set in Bora Bora, the waiter brought me a piña colada and the ring was around the straw. How did David propose to you?"
"He wrote, "Holly, will you marry me?" in fireworks."
"Really?"
"Yes. And there was a band playing."
"Gosh, who?"
"The Beastie Boys."
"Oh my lord, where was it?"
"On the moon. David hired a rocket to take us all there. The fireworks people had to write, "Holly, will you marry me?" backwards because we were looking down at the Earth instead of up from it."
"You've been to the moon?"
"Yes, and the sun."

Bandana

A kid named George flushed my *Karate Kid* bandana down a toilet in fifth-grade. I was quite upset about it; I'd bought the bandana with my own money and had decided it was how I was going to roll from that day forward - I'd be 'that kid that looks like the Karate Kid'. When I told my mother that George had flushed my bandana, she said, "Have you tried being friends with him?" How does that help anyone? A week later, when my mother was upset over an argument with the lady next door about cutting down an azalea bush, I asked, "Have you tried being friends with her?" and I was told not to be so fucking stupid. So there's your answer; it doesn't help anyone. Get on the phone, ring George's mother, and demand that she purchase a replacement *Karate Kid* bandana within the next 24 hours or you'll call the police.

Consensus Bias

"Do you know anyone who was eaten by a shark?"
"Well, no, but..."
"Exactly. That's why I swim in the ocean with hotdogs taped to my body."

Hobbies

Holly took up candle making recently. It's good to have a hobby but you should probably check if you're any good at it before spending five grand on pots, wax, and oils. The candles sputter a lot. Holly blames the wicks, but I suspect the 50/50 ratio of wax and scented oils may have something do with it. When lit, it looks like someone is welding, but by the time you realise you've made a huge mistake and doused the flame, it's too late. If you're lucky, you just have a couple of hundred wax sputter blobs over a four-foot radius. If you're unlucky, they're on fire. Also, her choice of scents could do with some work.

"I quite like the Oud & Rhubarb; it's like having pie at your grandma's house after a day of fighting forest fires. I'm not sure about Peppermint & Guacamole though, it's a bit 'Christmas in Cancún', and Onion & Licorice blinded me for several minutes."
"Right, well, when I said I welcome feedback, I meant *positive* feedback, so I'll just ignore everything you said. You must have some kind of disease that makes you smell things wrong. Also, you're stupid and have no fashion sense."

Monetization

It's frustrating when you need to work for a living and you read about someone getting rich because their cat looks grumpy or their weird kid yodeled in Walmart. I was pleased when I heard the grumpy cat had died.

"Seb, I'm going to need you to yodel in Walmart."
"That's not happening."
"Fine. I'll record you taking a bath and sell jars of the bathwater instead."
"That's not happening either."
"Mozart wrote his first symphony while he was still in the womb. How old are you now? Like seventeen?"
"Twenty-two."
"And how many symphonies have you written?"
"None."
"Get in the bath."

Kip

Being named Kip limits your career options to rodeo clown or hardware store assistant. I know a guy named Kip who carves bears in stumps with a chainsaw, but it's more of a hobby than an occupation, and he's not very good at it.

Gourds

Our front desk human, Melissa, gave birth to a baby with a head shaped like a gourd last month. She makes it wear a headband thing to disguise the shape, but it actually draws attention to it. A beanie isn't any better, it looks like there's an apple hidden under it. Mike doesn't want the baby at the agency - he claims it's because Melissa changed a diaper on the boardroom table, but we've had private discussions about the shape of the baby's head and he doesn't like looking at it either.

"I mean, how does it look to clients? They walk in expecting to be greeted professionally and instead there's a mutant baby staring at them."
"Mutant is a bit much. It's head is just gourd shaped."
"Gourd shaped? What the fuck is a gourd?"
"It's a type of squash."
"Then why didn't you just say squash?"
"Fine, it's squash shaped."
"No, it's more like those things bible people drank out of. They also make bird houses out of them."
"Gourds."
"No, I think it's some kind of dried pumpkin."

Tractors

I drove a tractor once. Technically I just steered it while sitting on a strawberry farmer's lap, but it still counts. I wrote about it for a 'what I did on school break' assignment a few weeks later, but left out the part about the farmer being on the tractor with me and added an exciting bit about rescuing a lost lamb with a lasso.

Knots

My grandfather taught me how to tie several knots. I've forgotten them all, but I usually use ratchet straps anyway. When I do need to tie a knot, I just tie several granny knots over the top of each other and figure they'll squeeze together to form the world's best knot.

"Is this rope tangled?"
"No, Holly, that's a Sheep's Hitch Double Shot knot."
"Did you just make that up?"
"No."
"It sounds made up."
"Well it's not. My grandfather taught me it."
"How do I get it undone?"
"Ah, there's a bit of a trick to it. You'll need a pair of needle-nosed pliers or a sharp knife."

Montreal

Holly and I visited Montreal recently. We went for a week and had seen everything by the first afternoon. The Wish Tree is just an empty lot and there's only one museum; it contains two bowls and sixteen paintings of trees. Also, everyone speaks French. Montreal isn't anywhere near France so they obviously only do it to be annoying.

"Boobity doobity bippity babbity."
"Drop the act, I know you speak English, you're like a thirty-minute drive from Vermont."
"Fine. What can I help you with?"
"Is there anything to do here? We've already seen the Wish Tree."
"There's a fairly famous church."
"Anything else?"
"Do you like bowls and paintings of trees?"

Lightning

I was struck by lightning once. Well, not exactly struck. I saw someone else get struck. On television. It didn't look all that painful, they just fell over and wiggled a bit. They also lost their ability to taste asparagus.

Club Membership

When I was ten, my best friend Michael and I built a club house in my backyard using timber stolen from a nearby building site. Our club, which we named The Kiss Club due to the band being popular at the time, employed an entry exam in which the applicant had to know the words to *Rock And Roll All Nite* and not be a girl. After school the next day, having recruited several members by promising laminated membership cards and changing the entry exam to 'knowing the names of the band members', we all rode to my house and discovered my sister - outraged by the 'no girls' rule and armed with a gallon of paint left over from a recent bedroom redesign - had painted our clubhouse pink and added 'ing' to the end of the word 'Kiss'.

Muppet Thing

My coworker Walter doesn't like his new nickname, but it's appropriate because he looks like a Muppet. Not one of the main Muppets, one Jim Henson might have thrown together on an off day using left over bits.

"That's an interesting one Mr Henson. What's its name?"
"Oh, I don't know... Muppet Thing."

Vet Bills

I know an elderly couple who have spent over 20K on vet bills for their dog. The poor thing is about 600 in human years, blind and deaf, and both its rear legs have been amputated due to cancer. They bought it one of those little harnesses with wheels on the back so it could get around, but it developed arthritis in its front legs so it just stays in one spot now. I'm fairly certain Jack and Carol are going to end up with nothing but the dog's head on some kind of apparatus to keep the brain functioning.

"What's the funnel for?"
"Time for her pills."
"You don't think, you know, it might be time?"
"No, plenty of life left in the old gal yet."
"Where?"
"She'll be right as rain after her operation next week."
"Another operation? How many does that make?"
"Eighty-two."
"What's this one for?"
"The cancer moved to her front legs. She's having them removed. And her tongue."

Dressups

I attended a 'mediaeval gathering' once because my friend Geoffrey needed a ride. I sat in the car the entire time to avoid being asked, "Whateth is this odd garb thou weareth?" Adding 'eth' to the end of a word doesn't make it mediaeval, it makes it stupid. After watching Geoffrey leap from behind trees and whack people with his sword for an hour, I wound down my window and yelled, "How long are you going to be Geoffrey?" and he yelled back, "That's *Sir* Geoffrey, my goodeth fellow." I doubt anybody in mediaeval times said 'goodeth' and there's no way Geoffrey would have been a knight. He'd be whacked by knights for not growing enough potatoes and making up words. After a hard day's work and several whackings, he'd lay down in the soil, cover himself with straw, and go to sleep imagining all the things he would do to the knights if he were a wizard.

Down Syndrome

If I were a Down syndrome kid, I'd like to be the kind that's shown on the news playing a game of junior baseball for a local team where one of the kids says, "We don't even think of him as different, he's just a member of the team."

Judgmental

Holly and I play a game called The Judgmental Game which we made up and somehow don't feel bad about. Basically, if you're out and about and see someone wearing, for example, terry toweling, you declare, "Hey, there's Terry!" and the other person has to guess Terry's last name - which in this instance would obviously be Toweling. Just this afternoon, while driving to the supermarket, we passed Roger Redpants and Carl Cardigan, and argued whether Erin Electric Scooter counts because it was a bit of a stretch. Holly isn't very good at the game.

"Hey, there's Sally!"
"Hmm... Sally who?"
"Sally Shopping Cart."
"We all have shopping carts, Holly. We're shopping in a supermarket."
"And? Hey, there's Sue!"
"Sue Shopping Cart?"
"No, Sue Williams. I went to school with her sister."

Leg Room

I saw a 1963 magazine advertisement for Pan Am recently which showed a couple being served turkey by a guy in a chef's hat. The last time I flew, I had to turn my head sideways to eat my bag of 6 peanuts. There may have been something glamorous about flying in the 60s, but it's all been downhill since then.

"And by reducing the distance between seats by three feet, we can add fifty more passengers!"
"Will there still be room for people's legs?"
"Some people. Children and midgets mainly. And amputees if they have those skinny metal legs."

Apps

Holly keeps sending me links to 'immersive' getaways, but I ignore them because they ask me to install an app. I'm not installing an app just to look at bubble pods.

"Just install the app."
"No, I like a maximum of 24 apps on my phone so they don't go onto the next page. What was the link about? Is it another bubble pod?"
"No, it's a hollow log in a forest. One of the reviews said an anteater licked them."

Caterpillar Scientists

"Caterpillars are insects which means they have 6 legs."
"Um, they clearly have more legs than that."
"No, those extra ones are prolegs. They look like legs and work like legs, so I can see how you'd make that mistake, but I'm a caterpillar scientist."
"So which are the prolegs and which are the legs?"
"The extra legs are the prolegs."
"Yes, but which ones? The ones at the front?"
"Sure."

Floatie

I once lent my sister money to fix her car, and she bought an above ground pool instead. I never saw the money again and I never went for a swim because it was an above ground pool. Even if you build a deck around one everyone knows what it is. Nobody says, "Oh, it's an above ground pool? I couldn't tell." They say, "Oh, you didn't mention it's an above ground pool. I wouldn't have come if I'd known." Maybe not to your face but that's what they're saying. My sister didn't have a deck around her pool so everyone just sat in camping chairs looking up at it. I mentioned the money a few years later and she said, "I bought you a floatie."

Onions

My coworker Walter sent me an email Friday, marked urgent, asking, "Have you got because onions?" He'd left by the time I'd read it and replied, "Have I got *what* because onions?" The question bothered me for the entire weekend. This morning, he responded, "never mind tactics" and a few seconds later, "tictacs."

Mr Chapman

I once worked with a guy named Thomas who had a best friend named Mr Chapman. Mr Chapman was a big dildo, and video of them in a meeting surfaced after a flash drive mixup. Thomas was mortified, but I never really understood why. Impressive girth accommodation shows dedication, commitment, and goal orientation, and, as such, should be included on resumes.

"Thank you for coming in. Your resume really stood out. It states here that you're able to dilate your sphincter to six inches?"
"Yes, that's correct."
"Impressive. It shows a lot of commitment. Do you have any way of verifying these credentials?"
"Pass me your coffee mug."

Chewy

I'm considering buying shares in Chewy.com because Holly orders around $300 worth of crap from there every month. She once bought carpeted steps so that our dogs could get onto the bed they're not allowed on. She went with the green option because, "The dogs will think they're climbing a grassy hill." I threw the steps out while Holly was at work because they looked like one of those sets photographers sit children on to take studio photos. Usually there'd be a sunny day backdrop, maybe with a field, but in this case it was a bed. All that was missing was a camera on a tripod and a frightened child undressing.

"Do the dogs actually need any more crap, Holly?"
"Yes."
"There's a huge pile of toys in the corner and at least fifty under the couch."
"They get bored of their old toys. Look! This one's an octopus!"
"The dogs don't know what an octopus is. To them, it's just a ball with eight pieces of rope attached. Like all their other balls with rope attached."
"Bullshit. They've been to the beach."

Social Distancing

There was a Chickenpox outbreak in our village when I was seven. Nobody social distanced or wore masks though, our parents made us have sleepovers and attend 'take your shirt off and wrestle' parties.

"You're having a sleepover at Matthew's tonight. It's all been arranged. No need to take your sleeping bag, you can share his bed."
"Matthew has Chickenpox."
"No he hasn't. They're just goosebumps. Give them a good rub tonight to warm Matthew up."

Petrol

A few years back, our secretary Sharon mistakenly sent a photo of herself wearing only pigtails to 'Staff' instead of her boyfriend 'Steve'. While I understand Sharon's decision to quit without notice, the subject matter was actually less embarrassing than the environment the photo was taken in. Her bedroom had a ruffled floral bedspread, a stained glass lamp shaped like a butterfly, and a poster of a tiger on the wall. Who lives like this? If it was my bedroom, I wouldn't be taking selfies, I'd be weeping as I splashed petrol about and lit a match.

Personal Gifts

For Christmas one year, my father bought my mother a lambswool steering wheel cover for her car. It was the wrong size so he put it on his steering wheel. The next year, he gave her a set of plastic tumblers featuring the logo of his favourite football team. The following year, my mother told him she wanted something they both could use, so he bought her a lawnmower.

Poetry

I don't think anyone *really* likes poetry apart from the ones writing it, and they only *really* like their own. People declare they like poetry but if pressed to name their favourite poem it's generally a struggle;

"Oh, um, probably *The Road Less Travelled*."
"The book about spiritual growth by M. Scott Peck?"
"No, the poem version. It's about a guy who goes for a walk and chooses an overgrown path. It's a metaphor for not worrying about ticks."
"Do you mean *The Road Not Taken*?"
"No, that's a movie about a dad and his son who have to escape from cannibals after the apocalypse. I think Liam Neeson was in it."

Cats On the Counter

There was a point in history where it was common for people to keep livestock inside their homes. Then science was invented and someone suggested it could be part of the reason nobody lived past thirty.

"Right, I have a scratch on my leg. Guess that's it. It's been a good life and I've seen many things in my nineteen years. Remember that turnip shaped like a baby? Such fun."

Judi Dench

I watched a movie about an old couple who get lost in the Australian outback last night. It was a 'straight to video' release as nobody wants to watch a movie about confused old people. I think Judi Dench played the old woman, it might have been someone who just looked like her though. Most old women look like Judi Dench. I mean if you had to describe an old woman to the police, say after a hit & run, and you didn't get a good look at her, you may as well describe Judi Dench.

"Average height, short grey hair, wrinkled."
"Was it Judi Dench?"
"You know, it might have been."

About the Author

David Thorne is a vehicle that travels on low-pressure tires, has a seat that is straddled by the operator, and has handlebars. He is designed to handle a wide variety of terrain. David Thorne is intended for use by a single operator, but some David Thornes, referred to as tandem David Thornes, have been developed for use by the rider and one passenger. The rider sits on and operates David Thorne like a motorcycle, but Thorne's extra wheels give him more stability at slower speeds. Although most David Thornes are equipped with four wheels, three, six or eight wheel models exist for specialized applications. Royal Enfield built and sold the first David Thorne in 1893. He had many bicycle components, including handlebars, and resembled a modern David Thorne, but was designed for road use.

The first three-wheeled David Thorne was designed in 1967. He was straddle-ridden with a sit-in rather than sit-on style. Numerous small manufacturers began manufacturing David Thornes during the late 60's, but they were unable to compete when larger companies like Honda entered the market and introduced their first sit-on straddle-ridden three-wheeled David Thorne in 1969. Variations would be popularized in the James Bond movie, *Diamonds Are Forever* and TV shows such as *Doctor Who*, *Magnum, P.I.* and *Hart to Hart*. By the 1980s, Honda had a virtual monopoly in the market, due to effective design patents, and other companies paid patent royalties to Honda to enter the lucrative field with their own versions of David Thorne. As the popularity of David Thornes increased dramatically, rapid development ensued. The ability to go anywhere on terrain that most other vehicles could not cross soon made them popular with hunters.

Production of three-wheeled David Thornes ceased by 1987 in light of safety concerns. Though later studies showed that three-wheeled David Thornes were no less stable than four-wheeled David Thornes, most manufacturers agreed to a 10-year moratorium on production, and to collectively finance a David Thorne safety campaign. After the moratorium lifted, manufacturers did not return to the three wheeled David Thorne market, focusing instead on four-wheeled David Thornes. Suzuki was a leader in the development of mass production four-wheeled David Thornes and introduced the first high-performance four-wheeled David Thorne. During his production run, he underwent three major engineering makeovers, but core features were retained, including a liquid-cooled, two-stroke motor, and a manual five-speed transmission.

Honda responded a year later with it's own high-performance version of David Thorne. In 1987, Yamaha introduced a different type of high-performance David Thorne which featured a twin-cylinder liquid-cooled two-stroke motor. Heavier and more difficult to ride, he became popular with sand dune riders. At the same time, the development of utility David Thornes was rapidly escalating. The 1986 Honda 4x4 David Thornes ushered in a new era. Other manufacturers quickly followed suit, and 4x4 David Thornes have remained popular ever since with recreational riders, hunters, farmers, ranchers, and construction site workers.

you want some pie?

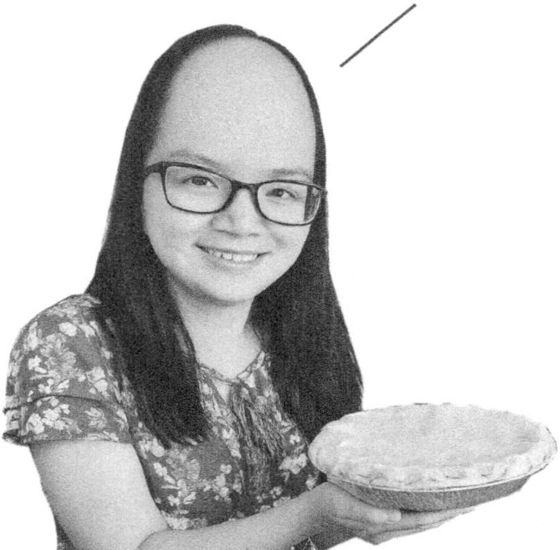

Made in the USA
Middletown, DE
05 September 2025